Disbelief

Also by John Ash

Casino
The Bed
The Goodbyes
The Branching Stairs

"We have modelled a world in miniature which exists only in these pages and is not to be found by the most enterprising geographer. Books which never were written are brought into being. People whom no one has ever seen sell their mythical wares undisturbed. Modern cities rise and flourish. Vast carnivals parade in sumptuous grandeur."

American Type Founders' Company: Catalogue of 1923

JOHN ASH

DISBELIEF

CARCANET

Acknowledgements

Grateful acknowledgement is made to the following publications where the poems first appeared. *The New Yorker*: Landscape with Artists, The Other Great Composers, Unwilling Suspension; *Paris Review*: The Monuments, A Long Encounter, Party Damage, In The Street; *PN Review*: The Hotel Brown Poems, Little Variations for Natalia Ginzburg, A Ship Called Snow White, Low-Flying Aircraft: An Eclogue; *Brooklyn Review*: Men, Women & Children; *Mudfish*: Surface Reversal, The Sudden Ending Of Their Dream; *New Poetry I: P.E.N. Anthology*: Memories of Italy, Epigraphs for Epigones, and The Wonderful Tangerines. The author would like to thank the Ingram Merrill Foundation and the Mrs Giles Whiting Foundation for their generous financial assistance.

First published in 1987 by
Carcanet Press Limited
208-212 Corn Exchange Buildings
Manchester M4 3BQ
and
198 Sixth Avenue
New York, NY 10013

British Library Cataloguing in Publication Data

Ash, John, *1948-*
  Disbelief.
  I. Title
  821'.914   PR6051.S3/

  ISBN 0-85635-695-6

The Publisher acknowledges financial assistance from
the Arts Council of Great Britain.

Typeset in 10pt Palatino by Bryan Williamson, Manchester
Printed in England by SRP Ltd., Exeter

Contents

Part I

Landscape with Artists
for David Kermani

This is not a river, but a limb of the ocean,
an arm outstretched to indicate
the great beauty of these mountains and woods,
all that they can mean to the amazed traveller –

and the bridges don't connect
so much as adorn, as red barns and white porches
adorn, improbably, the mild hillsides; these dead leaves,
the birch stems might have been
painted in Vienna or by the Attersee,
and people have come so far
simply to look and to understand a little, –
oh, only a fragment, a portion of this world
that is so distant and still can be touched
and still returns the touch somehow:

it is hidden but its trace lasts
like the things etched into you in childhood –
a porch, a stone dog, the colour of a shirt.

Unwilling Suspension

The cab should take off at this point
climbing straight over the river like a gull.
You can get so far but no nearer.
The island may be mirage or projection:
its towers remain on the horizon, –
the work of an ambitious child with scissors.
The bridges haven't been built, or they are
pitifully few. The roadway moans.

This is not The Good Place
and it assuredly is. In the evening
the sun makes it a glory
and deep in fissures, under fire-escapes,
are people who go hungry
and they seem to complain so little
they might be saints who had chosen
this way. Why have you come here?
It will not bring comfort, –
if you want that look somewhere else,
in the pages of an album or the far reaches of a park.

With oaths and hand gestures
the route changes: we shift north
passing between subsiding warehouses,
under obscure constructions of rusted girders,
discovering isolated houses with floral balconies,
carved doorframes. For some time we watch
elevators rising and falling in a distant building.

There needs to be a new religion of the city, –
a bible only of long-lined psalms
for long-lined buildings and their lights.

People sleep on the vents.
At night fireflies buzz the towers.
But we aren't getting any nearer
and how can I tell you how it feels
to spend an hour advancing by inches toward
something resembling a faded, theatrical curtain?

How can I tell you? The legends accumulate
like wealth or grain at the edge of a famine.
You will never be bored and you will never
conclude your investigations since the crime
has no culprit, or too many to fill the old courthouse.

The cab stalls on the far bank, its headlights ablaze.
I couldn't photograph any of this for you.
I couldn't show its reflection in a windshield.
I could tell you about the rain: it is not raining.

Memories of Italy
for Pat Steir

I loved the light of course
and the way the young men
flirted with each other.
I loved the light, –

the way it fell out of a sky like a painting,
or perhaps like the ground (if this
is not too paradoxical a way of
putting it) for a painting,

and the way the young men stood in the station
wearing jeans that were the colour of the sky
or the sea in a painting, jeans that revealed
the shapes of their legs which reminded me

of the statues in the square outside the station
where the light fell with such violence
their shadows were blacker than the despair of the painter
who cannot proceed with the painting: the canvas
is before him, its ground blue and blank as the sky above the station

where the young men loiter like the heroes in one of the lulls of
    the Trojan War
when lazy picnics were possible beside the calm sea, under the
    smiling sky,
and it half seems that the war will end forever, for surely they
    must all soon fall in love with each other...
And the painter knows his painting must be heroic, that the blue
    is not the sky
but a terrible sea a God has raised to drown the beauty of the
    young men in the marble battlefield of the station,

and he knows the painting is finished,
that it represents the envy the divine must feel
towards the human as marble must envy the sea,

and the painting is hung in the concourse of the station
and the young men drift indifferently to and fro before it:
their feet hardly seem to touch the blue marble ground.

The Other Great Composers
for Douglas Crase

They lived in places tourists don't care to visit
beside streams the obscure workings of local pride
insisted were rivers: there were willows or derelict mills
sometimes a boathouse with Palladian ambitions, –
in the backwoods, except that the towering pines were,
often as not, replaced by clusters of factory chimneys, –
isolate, the factories gone, the chimneys octagonal,
grand as columns remembering a Trajan victory
although severely unadorned. They lived in places where
commerce destroyed the Roman forts, the common fields
with red viaducts, canals now, like them, disused
and forgotten, depositories for ignorance, or else
they sank into the confines of a half-suburban dream
of pastoral they couldn't share: the works grew longer,
"unperformable"... The aggression of the ordinary,
the tepid love expressed in summerhouses too small
really to contain lover and beloved, the muted modes
and folksongs rediscovered, dead as elms, drove them
to new forms of learning and excess, ruthless
distortions of the academic tones and tomes,
chords that decayed over long bars into distances
where bell-hung, bird-haunted pagodas of their own
design rose up, tier on tier, to radiant mountains, –
mountains from which they confidently expected,
year after year, the arrival of the ancient and youthful
messenger who would confirm the truth of these visions.
It is impossible yet to say that they were wrong:
the music is unproved and undisproved; their operas
require cathedrals in which the angels and grotesques
come alive for one scene only; their fugues and toccatas
demand the emergence of a pianist eight-handed
like a Hindu god whose temples remain a sheaf of sketches,
whose religion is confined to a single head, maddened
or happy, dead-centred in a continent of neglect.

American Uncles

Like anyone else
the prisoners will enjoy the Ghent Band concert,
and Dido the dog will put her nose where she wants,
in spite of reprimands or yelping prudes.

The band ditches Offenbach for a Gershwin tune.
That Ghent girl handles her baton
with such a Slavic passion,
you just have to love her
and the day. The mildness of the afternoon
and the expectation of champagne
descends upon the little town
like a favorite uncle's
calming hand.

Behind the courthouse, the prison's quiet
in expectation of a blue refrain.

The rose-trees stand to attention
on either side the path,
each one a blue-eyed cadet.
They are perhaps too yellow? Too pale?
Sometimes you'd like to muss them up
a little. But leave them be. I think that they,
too, are enjoying the concert somehow,

and they look good from the netted veranda
where we're drinking the first wine of the day.

Now it remains for us
to drive into autumn's ravines,
into fiery colours and urgent music.

Come on. Say yes.
It's only a short walk to the garage.

Croissant Outlets in Seattle

"...je suis dévoué à un trouble nouveau, – j'attends
devenir un très mechant fou."

There are still more hairs on my head
that there are croissant outlets in Seattle.
People tell me I'm looking good, but should I believe them?
Is anyone more trustworthy than a newspaper?

The tour of inspection has begun –
how exhausting it is –
and many there are who come seeking favours.
The reports pile up and the figures muddle me.

I feel childish but refuse assistance:
the last malfunctioning latrine must be registered.

In the dispiriting afternoons of these parts
I retire to the sheds behind the house
to work on the system I have devised which,
in time, will flood with unbearable light
the face of the nation: those wattled jowls

that still refuse to register, in even
the lowest key, one true emotion.

There are many now in minks who will be
exiled, perhaps to the Aleutians.

Ah bays and bridges! Towns, tunnels, ghettoes and gulfs!
Delicatessens and corporate headquarters!
Volcanoes, phonebooths and parking lots!
You will not escape my hand.

Is a tower of evil less evil because night
covers it with diamonds? Beautiful cankers
you will seem more like a poem
when I am through: you will be perfect roses,
innocent as the first day, installed
at all points of the city, like fountains
in the Turkish city of Bursa.

15

But it is too much for one man to do,
even if he had a good woman behind him,
and this is not the nineteenth century
of novels and puddings, of novels *like* puddings...

I regard the world as a TV
on which I change channels at will,
never moving from the bed:
everything must be in the place
where I can stare it in the face.
And I can't bear
for anyone to run
her fingers through my hair.

I will abolish the boudoir and the changing room;
there will be no more evening dresses or perfume!

Today the Union of the Mothers of Seattle
came bearing a petition, and they cried, –

"Oh save us! Install a priest as governor!
For the world seems to unravel like skirts
about our feet. The bread we buy is stale,
even before it leaves the store,
and good tomato paste cannot be discovered
anywhere in the state. Therefore
we come bearing a large cheque
which is yours if you will only
dispel this state of uncertainty

like the mist that never lifts from the summits
of our city's over-reaching towers.
Oh our city, lying beside its beautiful,
uninscribed pages of water and light!
Indeed we are littered like dry grasses
amid the play of water and light,
so, in our extremity, we come to you
with withered hands..."

Ah Seattle, Seattle,
with your boats and bridges and spires,
and your charming spruces,
I imagine you are like Norway.
You *will* be like Norway.

Already I see your vertiginous fiords,
the wooden houses of Bergen,
the profound dramas of your meagre households,
and over all is the pervasive odour
of herrings. But there remains
the matter of revising the folksongs.

Party Damage

The invitations were returned
or people arrived on the wrong evening,
so your worst fears were fulfilled
and you sent the singers home, still in costume.
The weather changed and changed again.
The hospital was a kind of inverted cake
with white, glazed icing dripping from its eaves.

It is as natural that confusion
and anxiety should be our companions
as it is that old women should complain
in pharmacies; yet some things should be clear
as summer's red sail turning in the bay.

"Please understand I mean exactly what I say,
no more." A word is spoken, an ordinary word,
and it becomes an entire landscape, –
an open and illustrated city: you might be
alone in a desert at noon with nothing
but the mirage of a Pepsi Cola sign to guide
your feet, or penniless on Fifth Avenue
without even a scarf to sell as Christmas approaches, –
or else you are the young prince in his walled paradise
idly shooting song birds with a jeweled arrow.

Please return the arrow: I think I put that jewel there.
Don't harm the animals or birds. Leave
heaven or hell out of consideration.
Certain things are, in the end, unforgivable
though it may take years for this to be noticed,
like a red stain pressing through a wall.

"The other day I was walking up an avenue, –
I forget its number, – when I saw the word SAVE
written in skywriting far above the city.
I am not making this up: it happened."

18

The House Comes to Rest in its Garden
for Darragh Park

Sitting on the back porch with the painter and his dog
you remark the absence of car-alarms or voices yelling in Spanish,
then later find your sleep disturbed
by the stentorian exchanges of bullfrogs: yes,
the pond is inhabited and not so natural as it looks.

After nine months freezing and stewing in the city
you could make a fool of yourself out here. You might say –
"How perfectly the house fits its setting, how it seems
to snuggle down into its hillock like a dog into a sofa –
why, it seems to have grown up out of the place
like its graceful neighbour, the butternut tree!..."

And how wrong you'd be! The whole house
was ordered in 1912 from *Sears & Roebuck*,
one of how many hundred editions of the same design,
and delivered in numbered parts by train. And it is hard

to imagine the distant town, clamped down under the rain,
where the walls and the windows, the roofs and the doors
were made, or their long, crated journey and the hurried assembly.

In those days people didn't just ship their houses out to the island,
they shipped their winter lives out into the summer,
bringing fat armchairs, elaborate drapes, classic libraries
and pianos no one played much, as little inclined
to accommodate themselves to the heat as Viceroys in the tropics,
and yet it was sea breezes that drew them from the city.

Are you disappointed by what you have learnt,
disappointed to find the marks of artifice and industry
where you expected nature? Not really,
for this unexpected information enhances, rather than spoils
your first grateful response to the sight of so many
different kinds of green surrounding an oval mirror of water,
and the garden, too, is a work of art that conceals art.

It looks almost wild, or at least like an uncropped field,
until you notice the new plantings which will compose themselves,
at the right season, into careful designs of pale blues and yellows,
purples and the pink of swamp-roses. It will be lovely.
It *is* lovely. An elliptical enclosure
of privet and honeysuckle (both now in pungent flower)
widely surrounds the butternut's swooping branches,
and you don't feel enclosed in any crowding sense
for gaps have been left in the hedge
through which a mass of chrome-yellow flowers will show,
and even on days when it is clouded or raining

sunlight will seem to fall steadily there –
a promise it would be too harsh to call false.

A Ship Called Snow White

On a light breeze through branches and the sounds they make

Something remembered arrives at this suburban platform

You can't say what it is but the sun knows a chapter or two of it

Perhaps a whole book could be written on the shadow of these
palings

Will the light stay on all night and the moon sail through clouds?

The timetables are punctuated by snowstorms delayed by breakfast
drowsiness

But the advancing front of the train is like the sun (yellow I meant
to say)

I could stay here till morning if the ticket-vendor talked more

Departure and ensuing emptiness are agreeable if correctly
observed

You haven't slept with anyone for weeks and you realize it doesn't
matter

No clocks strike this hour and its singular transparency can't last

The lines sing above the pitch of hearing at the level of the highest
branches

Will the light stay on all night conserving shadows and graffiti?

Will it sail through clouds (the moon) like a ship called Snow
White?

Mucking About in the Fountain
for Bernard Padden

How to advance out of the mess of play, leavings of a memorable night?

Even if it is the last scene of *Chrysanthemums* (a drama) the curtain still refuses to descend, and while we chat and glance, too distracted to notice the way these momentous events unfold like crumpled wings, the furniture is moved about.

There is nowhere to sit down. The youth at stage left waves a long sleeve and mouths words that never reach us. We are still waiting. Yes, it's often like this...

The props are transparent, transparent and cold, even in the scene representing the Garden of Summer and the Garden of Fand, yet there is something human in it all, an imitation of our gestures that goes beyond mere "wishing on a star," and despite the possibly false "air of sophistication" the gauzes do not confuse the issue, even as the view of tenements and a bell tower is swept away during the brief span of a drink.

The banner of song unfurls: EVERYTHING MUST CHANGE

and real rain begins to fall from the ceiling. Umbrellas are raised. A wind molests the Hyacinths. Leaves fall in showers, and the old actress advances, first clearing a space with her foot, to give us the lessons of her years:

"Always wear gloves...I remember we stayed up all night for a week sewing our costumes. I was Saint Theresa. I wore a white gown which, in certain lights, appeared gold. Yes, it was good to be alive in that year even as the telegrams arrived, laden with the griefs of all our kind."

With such wisdom, such history and set design it will be apparent we lack for nothing.

The lights are dimmed. A knowledgeable hum rises from the crowd. Night pours from a vast pothole bordered by wild festoons: "Aw shucks!" it seems to say. Portentous, preludial, the

22

cedar engulfs the sun-dial. The light from a star meets the gleam on the wrist-band of your watch. But it has all become like the eighteenth century. No one can sit still during the long recitatives and arias which are beautiful but out of date as Handel's once were. An overweight castrato holds the stage. Let's take a walk...

in the restricted but attractive dimensions available. Some limits are useful like the rim of a dance-floor or box hedges that direct the lines of sight towards an octagon, a rose-cloud or a word, – the word "intention," for example, or the word "avoidance." This is nothing more than a foyer of course, and the design of the whole is clear in our minds like a nerve-system, but we can induce forgetfulness enough to enjoy all the build-in surprises. So we can sob when the messenger falls by the lake crying out that the musical has failed somewhere in the desert of the provinces. The audiences in Irkutsk aren't what they used to be.

A general march past ensues. A few lines of dialogue remain trembling on the air like Chinese kites: "Dearest, for shame!"... "So it was you all the time!"... "Waiter, this lemonade is warm."... Also half a scene or two, – hardly more than skits or sketches – cluttering the sward like tatters of a giant balloon. And the lesson of the years, the lesson of the shadows (of those who vanished into them) is resumed:

"I'm afraid you were all bad pupils, inattentive, always mucking about in the fountain that was the focus of our little court like a Sun-King. You don't understand the forms, – how each was a triumph over sorrow and oppression, – but this doesn't alter the affection I feel for you, and must continue to feel if my heart still beats: you who were changed by me as a city is by the songs it has written. The horizon is clear and simple as a diagram in the geometry you learnt in school. You have no choice but to move toward it as if towards the only gate in an endless wall. Little barbarians, understand at last that everything we see is artificial, even the closed mouth of the person you desire above all others, – not *forever*, but for the time they fill your sight like a carved chair-back, a heap of sun-bleached books, a tub of blue flowers obstructing the mottled mirror, the marbled sky: true ends and objects of this slandered guest which last as long as the senses are unexhausted."

Becoming a Berceuse

This is not exactly what I mean.
It is all approximate things, –
Dull landscapes and duller loves
Which in this secretive, apathetic air
Cannot have clear edge or colour.

Perhaps another climate is required?
So a man you met at a party
Writes to you tardily: "I wish I could be more
Enthusiastic." And you also wish it,
You wish you could be too.

It all derives, circumstantially,
From unwise attention given to ideas
That no doubt govern your life,
As grinding seasons turning,
Obscurely and exactly, but are so much
Degraded they must be ignored

Steadfastly like mouths and eyes
With drunken promises at parties.
For example, the wrong government
Has been elected. It is atrociously
Wrong, but it is useless to smash
The TV because of this,

And how can you, in your confusion,
Revise these numbers and these processes?
Babylonian darkness is too grand
A concept, so, a world of *quavering*
Littleness, unwonted dimness and cold

Of a day in June, no balconies,
No view, no enchantment
Fallen from the air above mountains
Nameless mountains which you
Or a figure resembling
A scrambled signal sent from you

Kept approaching and approaching
Along the ruined corridor
Of last night's serial dream:
But to reach the mountain
Or to reach the fountain
May mean nothing, –
Coach parties and the corpses of businessmen.

Probably your dreams
Aren't important. However
I think your friends
Are. And their praise

No matter how much you have formed them
Or how heedlessly this happened,

And the night in which you are awake
When no messengers arrive
Braying refusal or acceptance,
When you consider the idea of sleep
As a theorem, and you do not succumb, –
You resist as you would any
"Received opinion,"

Any conventional rose
Or amorous declaration, –
And the thought of numberless
Bodies forgotten in sleep
Surrounds you like a net

Whose filaments
Are extension, not confinement,
Bossed with stars,
Becoming a berceuse

So vastly dispersed
None can hear it whole.

From Lorca's Letters

What can I say of my song?

It must have the blurred charm
of an overheard conversation, –
something like the scent of a flower
hidden in snow, in the distance.

It must have the melancholy
of these canals and towers,
the clarity of this plain where
autumn polishes its red knives...

What can I say of my song?

In a century of typewriters and stupid deaths
we must learn to love the moon
above the lake of our souls, –
the oriental moon and the purple mosquitoes,
the dew that descends for the dead.

*

The other day I studied my past attentively.
It was not mine. I saw my thousand selves
stretched out in time's attics forever
and a white dust like powdered sugar covered them.
My mother, death, had given me the rusted key,
and for a second I understood *everything*...

*

The world is a shoulder of dark meat –
black flesh of an old mule –
and the light is on the other side
where there are sonorous spikes of wheat
and white processionals of clouds.

I embrace you and the horizon rises,
constructed like a great aqueduct,
and amid the chalk roses and canna-lilies of Egypt
the city of Alexandria raises towers
like stems of crystal and reddish salt.

The first snows have fallen. The yellow begins,
infinite and deep, to play with twenty shades of blue.

★

Since the weather is mild
the young ladies of Granada
climb to the whitewashed terraces
to look at the mountains.
(They do not look at the sea.)

The blondes go out in the sun.
The brunettes stay in the shade.

Those with chestnut hair remain in first-floor rooms
looking into mirrors, adjusting little celluloid combs.

And you will wet your braids in the sea
while the stuttering song of the motor-boats comes and goes,
and when you stand in the doorway of your house
sunset will light up the coral that the virgin holds in her hands.

How quiet it is! Only the stuffed bear
keeps you company. The maid has gone to the dance.

But now, for you alone, the two black dancers,
dressed in green and white crystal, will dance
the sacred dance of the windows and the door.

Memory sits in an armchair
eating cakes, drinking dark wine.
Under the white porticoes
an accordion is heard.

★

Now it occurs to me to write a comedy
whose chief characters are photographic enlargements,

those people we see in doorways, –
newlyweds, sergeants, dead girls,
anonymous crowds of moustaches, wrinkles, and hats...

and in the midst of all these people
I will place an authentic ghost, –

Marianita dressed in white, her hair loose,
sewing the flag of Liberty.

★

Here are some postage stamps
I have unearthed from your favourite century.

I don't know, Melchorito,
who these respectable gentlemen might be.

They seem to be musicians. *Are* they musicians?
Surely these are nights of Italian opera
and snow-covered roof-tops? Voices like diamonds
and fountains, orchestras of vaporous silk...

The young man in his heavy overcoat,
half a Roman and half a professor of literature,
must have died young, I think: consider his smile.

And the young woman looking through her glasses,
for a closer view of the handsome tenor,
doesn't wear a white crinoline
as some, heedless poets might suppose.

You need only look at her brow to know
that this lady of illusions is dressed in the colour of bone,
and carries a skull crowned with roses in her hands.

The others eat home-made bread, watered
with the characteristic tears of the epoch.

★

Look closely at the *very spiritual*
photograph I have sent you. Notice

that I appear in a light like that of a murder scene,
or a dark corner where a delicate pickpocket
stashes his bundle of bills. See how capriciously

the lens reveals the slack harp
looming at my back like a jelly-fish.

The whole atmosphere partakes somehow
of the last twitchings of cigar ash.

★

A green moon wearing a purple halo
Appears above the blue mist of the Sierra Nevada

At twilight we live in a half-erased dream
Everything slowly evaporates
We're left in a desert of rose and dead silver

Our flesh hurts from so many bright stars
In India the nights are not more aromatic

The face of the town turns pale
And in the streets that open toward the fields
There is the murmur of an abandoned harbour

In front of my door
A woman sang a lullaby
Like a ribbon of gold
Extending to the limits of the world

Ah little carnation
Of the most secret path . . .

I love the clear water and the turbid star.

A Lithuanian Mantilla

The night is clear.
The cows are in the byres.
The books are bound in quires.
Great stars appear,
and in the city of a hundred tottering spires
they are lighting festal fires, –
they are stringing lights on wires
all across the central square
and no one tires of this affair, –
the chance to vent suppressed desires
in huge chaotic choirs.

But dark mists rise from mires
in fetid corners of the shires
and men whom no man hires
fume with fury and despair
declaring: "It's unfair, –
though each of us aspires
to sing a sweeter air
to shame the mansions of the squires,
how can we go dancing in the square
with no better prospect near
than dumbly sitting here?
For us these fires
bring no more cheer
than funeral pyres."

The city walls are sheer,
the flames like spires,
and the people dancing there
have immolated fear:
their lying bards are bashing lyres.
This crowd acquires
only good news from the town criers.

In his high chamber the Emir
prances under a chandelier
with the wife that he admires
more than marriage quite requires.

Beyond the gates in darkness drear
a foppish cavalier
is caught in tangled briars.
Underneath the moonlight's glare
lines of masochistic friars
wander in an atmosphere
dismal as towns in Delaware.
Vast herds of deer. The stars austere.
Buildings designed by Albert Speer.

And the people in the square
declare: "We are debonair,
each one of us a millionaire.
Beneath these splendid portières
we dance untouched by fear or care."
They are not liars,
but people warmed by festal fires
rarely think of what transpires
when sunlight burnishes the spires:
the dancer tires
and every fire expires.

The Wonderful Tangerines

1

Taking one's head off
is an odd way of showing
appreciation of the symphony,
but this is what she has done, –
the woman with the pastoral,
Marie Antoinette air
holding her smiling head
on a level with her hips,
and the guests murmur: "Charming.
So clever. I suppose it is done
with mirrors." But of course
it isn't. Strange to look
down on one's hat while
it is still on one's head.
The symphony is one of those
with picturesque titles, you know, –
The Claw-Hammer, The Flight-Bag,
The Spaniel, and so on...

2

"My dear I must tell you
about the cutlery.
None of it would match
and believing that music,
in propitious circumstances,
can alter the shape of
material objects, he placed it
in a transparent plastic
container next to the piano.
The concerto was a wild success
but still the supper was a shambles."

3

For the rhapsodies
we arranged the grapes
in violin cases
under the German busts.

The members of the quartet concealed themselves
behind black curtains, only their hands
protruding through the narrow apertures provided.
The string emerged slowing from their cuffs.

They began with a lyrical andante
(composed by the principal string-master)
– slender, variously tinted threads
gently attenuated amid the eight, gesturing
hands. The effect was most poignant,
and they ended with the awesome counterpoint
of a Grosse Fugue, a mesh
so dense it might be mistaken
for topiary. When a volunteer
finally mounted the platform
to pull a single, trailing strand
and the entire, immense structure
collapsed before our eyes
the applause was tumultuous.

4

It is November.
Cloud-shadows scud across
the shallow lake water,
and the Duke moves sadly
towards the bathing huts.
It is too late in the season to swim
but this is not his intention.
He approaches a pale, once royal-blue,
much-weathered bathing hut
and enters. He kneels down
at the centre of the little room
and raises his eyes towards the far wall.
Nailed to it are six complete
and luxurious sets of women's lingerie,
a honeyed beige in colour.
There is a space on the right
for a seventh set. He reaches
in his pocket and brings out
the long, gleaming nails. A tear
forms in his eye.

Epigraphs for Epigones

An inrush of children
turned the upper decks into an aviary.
From that vantage
we could see orange and mauve sweetpeas
obscuring the weathered sections of a fence.
There was hideous singing
and violent assertion of character
in the courteous face of death
who descended the stairs, not wishing
to cause embarrassment, now or hereafter.
The rails were smudged with dust, and also
the several petals of the suburb
wilting like gloves
in the average torpor, in the muffled shrillness
that spoke of the need to choose
another scene.

The old violin case. The head of hair.
Crushed fruit. The faces drawn on paving stones.
A deer park or sailing boat. Letters
in the rainswept journal telling
of the ridiculous passions that convince,
are all that convince... All these could be part of it
as long as they have the backing of a breeze
just starting up, gently, but fresh, indisputable
as dying or the pathos of evening traffic passing
below the city towers with a sound like catarrh:
all will be included in the new proposals
that really will be pasted up on the walls and the arches
someday soon, believe me! For now

the trivial journey with the shopping bags and children,
along canal banks crowded with the hope of salvation
must continue, –

but think only of departure,
the clouds you will be lost in
and let your irresolution be a law.

Observe how the tired objects of the day,
living like trees, seem to shift with their desire
to be ornamental in their final moment.

The Cascades N.Y.

I was inventing the waterfalls of the city,
dropping them behind the tables and chairs,
behind the strange moving staircases
they have in this place, beside
the counters selling fifty-dollar shirts and...

I was also arranging the ferns
and young businessmen about them –
the latter in place of outmoded Apollos,
and I had just got to women in fedoras when –

I can't tell you how angry I became,
it was like a storm –
the cabdriver helping himself to my cigarettes an' all...

when the weather forestalled me: there is
simply too much of it here –
it came in over the towers like perdition,
like a paragraph in the densest type
containing sentences boding no good,
none at all, and ill written to boot! The avenues
protested, vomiting trash into the deluge;
the manholes fumed. A woman stood and stood
on a corner waving a folded newspaper,
that drooped as it was drenched, desperate
for immediate transportation; you could say
hers was an extreme statement of the permanent
condition of the people in this place.

Rooflines and Riverbells
for Laura Nyro

Some evenings
there are no other songs
that so open the possibility
of summing the whole thing up, –

the smoke-rings and sleeplessness
in one, low chord on the piano,

and in one voice all the echoes
from subways stacked to the end
of the night-gutters are caught.

There's no room to generalise in, –
no room in a diamond
– the tears in the runnels wash that out to sea,
beyond the narrows and islands. Still

loneliness falls again and again
like rain. The night is moonfull
and the protagonist loathes the room

or grieves over it, grieves
over the music in wall-clocks and fire-escapes,
the cascade of bedsheets, the smoke
riding through the tassles of the lamp,
through brown hair in the mirror, –
the face always there in the left-hand corner
like a muddy stain, deriding the comb's
slow progress. A blue light spreads out

above the city like a new cloth
for a cancelled dinner-engagement,

and the veined, orange flowers at the centre
can't hold their petals any longer:
it can't go on like this in tricks and tracks.

In a theatre of dead leaves
you guess at things.
Were the streets kind? Who brought
white lavender? How fast were the clouds?
Did the gravestones stand up straight?
What fever burnt those eyes?

It feels like falling. It feels like dying.
It feels like religion, and we're trapped in this dream,

listening to the night wind,
to rain in the rivers,
rain on the girders of the bridges.

Doves fly from the white, docked liners.
There's coke and kisses in the roof-garden
where the dusty plants trail down dying,

and the single voice multiplies:
everything becomes an echo of itself, silvered.

The city's a mist of money
and the stunned lights signal love.

Forget the broken promises, the loss
of the wider sky, the paper
angels' wings hung up back stage.

To Illustrate the Day

and how it feels, think of the house as a ship
or a small fleet of boats;
the wooden terrace rests lightly on the ground
ready to sail away into the distance;
the lawn is a still lake surface
and the shadows, lengthening from fir trees
to hedge, engulf the white garden furniture
which only glows more whitely as if
it had held back some of the light
for its own special purposes: you wouldn't
sit on the benches at this hour, in this season.

   To illustrate the day,
try to adopt the simplicity of form
visible in the barns and houses;
follow the short arcs of birds above them;
so the robins here, compared to robins back home,
seem the size of hens, and the green heron
shivers nervously on the railing of the bridge;
its long head turns in a field of perception
very remote from yours: if it should see you
it would not recognise what it saw.

   To illustrate the day,
walk beside the ocean where the bluefish
multiply on the sand;
be adopted by a friendly dog
that peers at passing cars as if each
contained the object of its devotion;
don't fail to notice the dragonfly dead
in the dust or blown sand at the road's edge,
or the branches huddled in heaps
where the storm has passed, as if a week
of bonfires and festivities were planned
with lanterns suspended in willow trees.

Paint pale gold at the base of the sky;
dilute blues gradually, moving upwards and out,
through layers of green and brown and gold
from narrow enclosures the years contrived.
Over Sagg Pond at last the day is fading.

The Second Lecture:
An over-excited man tells us about some clouds
for Eugene Richie

This time really look at them. Don't take them for granted as they come in from the west driven against the watertanks. They are sweeping against the immense surfaces of the buildings, bringing rain to this city of verticals and grid-irons, shuddering the blinds. They come in wisps, in scarves at first, draped around the highest towers with, – how can I put it? – an air of innocence, nonchalance, even elegance as if a flapper were throwing on a stole before going out to find a romance of roses, diamonds and cabs. But they darken and grow denser. (She grows older; she throws on heavy furs and the temperature is dropping: soon winter will be here with its griefs, its careless deaths.)

The clouds become dense like certain textures in Brahms or the opening bars of Schoenberg's *Pelleas et Melisande*, and the river, the Palisades begin to fade, become ghostly under their pressure. Indeed, the clouds begin to resemble the kind of oppressive moral concepts that are indifferent to sensual detail (the flowers or toys, benches, fountains or parasols) and proceed on their way reducing everything, – life or landscape – to density and uniformity. And the faces of the buildings change. They become fearful, abashed, – if such a thing can be imagined. But perhaps it cannot and it may be that to speak of clouds, even the most ominous rainclouds, in this way is to moralise even in the process of disavowing moralism. Let us consider instead their formation and movements, their lyrical tendency to mass and disperse like civilizations in their rise and fall. Also I should speak of their architecture which varies from the most severe (hardly more than an infinite, blank wall) to extravagant baroque, – a heaven of balanced asymmetry with porticoes, colonnades, entablatures, shattered architraves, collapsing finials...Sometimes it happens that a grand avenue will open in the clouds above you, and though you may be walking along the finest avenue on earth, bordered by trees, luxury hotels, fashionable cafés and the mansions of millionaires it will fade in comparison to this transient splendour assembled out of suspended water vapour, – the uncounted droplets of the upper air!

41

These vistas are like music and have about them the insubstantiality that music must have for those who cannot read a score: the beautiful or disturbing sounds are there for some minutes or some hours, then they are gone, – you may never hear them again. A terrible anxiety grips you, for this great architecture, this great poetry consists only of transient vibrations of the air. A final chord brings both consummation and loss. Or so it must once have been. We are less anxious now that a performance may be preserved and reproduced, almost to infinity. It is not so with clouds which time governs absolutely. There is no remission or exemption. They mass and they disperse. They are, as Shelley said of autumn leaves, "like ghosts from an enchanter fleeing." But if an enchanter is involved we must imagine some very severe, self-lacerating magician who will never repeat exactly any of his enchantments, – an enchanter who drives himself on into the unknown, ever dissatisfied, unappeasable in his desire for new forms, "new flowers" (to refer to Flaubert) who, in order to conform to the demands of his exacting aesthetic, must destroy each creation at the point of its completion. So our lives are canopied by vast accumulations and disintegrations. The enchanter (who does not exist) passes his shimmering hands over and over our heads as if determined to heal us. But unlike us he will not die. We are effaced. A chrysanthemum of air remains poised to drop its petals into the blue that will reshape them endlessly.

Yesterday's Snow

Yesterday's snow
invents a new topography today, –
a system of lakes and rivers in spate
where once there was only a sheet of graph-paper
some of us had scrawled on confusingly.

You can't clean up this mess
you just have to wait for it to go away
like a headache. This is the aftermath
of the afternoon of a day without a morning.

Without mourning
or valediction either, God willing.
O powers, authorities and jokes,
Zinc lozenges and rumours of deaths!
I hear the voices of lost friends, –
vivid and fugitive as the scent of grasses
on an island where the sun was born.

Clouds move on.
I am already nostalgic for that moment
yesterday when I fell asleep at the party,
a pile of shrimps lying in rosy death on a plate in my lap.

My head's like a millstone underwater
but I raise it all the same.
My mouth is at the mouthpiece. One
by one I check on my friends: they are all *still there.*

A sigh heaves, big as a mountain.
Gosh! I am no longer sad,
as the whole of Europe is somehow sad today,
weeping under the escutcheon of a frozen clock.

Part II

Men, Women, and Children
for my brother Nicholas

Say that life is a festive marching to no purpose
other than to assert that we are all here
with the old jokes and "deviations from the norm,"
the embroidered Union-banners of self, –
that the silence which falls on us unexpectedly
is the shimmering silence of a theatre foyer
while the performance is in progress,

and it seems some quiet, backwoods drama
of upright pianos and reticent avowals is involved . . .
but the spectacle, with all its noise and patent
absurdity is "in our blood," and as the march continues
we meet friends and strangers with flashing smiles:
there is a band and the singing is defiant
but with a tendency to break up into laughter
as a wave shatters into diamonds, until

we are forced to think of our destination, –
the oppressive portals of the capitol,
the altars still smelling of blood.

Soul Music

Like the young
Aretha Franklin

the boy looked at his feet,
needlessly ashamed.

Imagined applause
thundered down streets

like crevices in crumbling brickwork,
and the real bricks crumbled,
the stones were losing their shape, –

stones of the doorway,
stones of the stairway,
stones of the lintel and the arch...

Perhaps the city would soon drain away
into the canals, the rivers and the sea
that daily sent its gulls to remind him
of its coldness and its closeness?

There was no kindness in the man sprawled
in the hallway, singing like a saw,
his one bandaged leg blocking all passage.

He was only looking for a home of some kind
but couldn't find it anywhere on the maps
the city authorities had set up in bus shelters.

At the excavations they discovered
a shopping precinct under the shopping precinct.

To his father
the sports pages were scripture
to which he offered the incense of a foul
tobacco; his mother sang to him, –
old songs of a reduced inheritance

Nothing said live,
nothing said hope, –

so the boy was lost for many years
and no one could trace him
even in landscapes constructed out of music,

until a voice, summoning
slandered histories, sprang out
like a tree from which the wind
stripped petals without depletion.

New Effusions of the Celtic Soul
for Billy Mackenzie

It's when we're listening a difference
is waiting in stated layers. You get confused.
Experience is a flail of stinging lights
wielded by whose hand? Is distraught singing
the drums annihilate. Best to start again
without those who've heard from some
near-neighbour or close acquaintance
of "The Solution" which, in truth, erases only and forever.

Tall orders are in order. And ardors: having
changed so many lives you must now change yours, –
pelted with promises, driven into the city
your desire has raised in steps like a ziggurat,

But take another look and you know,
with a certainty like a concrete wall,

it is all photographs ripped from the ancient brochure
in the waiting room, and the doctor still can't diagnose
your ague or itch. Those skyscrapers are pale blue paper,
their coronets tinsel, and your studies, however beautiful
the summer nights they occupied, like forgotten *Tafelmusik*
don't amount to much. These are foils and diversions,
though essential ones, and as this is written or read –
nearly identical activities really – we are inhabited
like an embassy by ghosts programmed to repeat us,

helplessly and at random, god knows how many
years in the future: the result must be embarrassment.

Reconsider everything now, like a plea hastily dismissed,
before it is too late, as it always is, and the trap-door opens.

That "difference," perhaps the reward of long waiting,
may be all that is aimed at: a displaced accent in the score,
a straying tendril in the on-going miracle of polyphony

which suddenly catches and snaps the wandering structure of
    the years
back into wholeness and purpose like the reaffirmation of an old
    friendship.

Nothing is routine or nothing needs to be,
and the variegated voices rise up (as they must)
drowning these concerns, asking only that you listen.

Nostalgia
for Harry Mathews

I am tired of Paris today, –
its books and sad flesh;
too much has happened here
and the intellectuals are dying.

In the stunned streets uniforms
obstruct the free movement of the citizens,
and the revolutionary thunder
has departed from the pianos;
the serenade is interrupted, –
alas! in the land of Claude Achille

one feels like an orphan crying in a yard,
dreaming of the bottom of the Seine, –
and this on a day when Leopold Senghor
is fitted for his Academie Française suit.

"I don't want to be immortal," I said at the airport,
"I just want to wander in your Elysian Fields."
But that was before the forgotten structuralist
declared her crushing love in a cloud of vile scent.

Not horns of the Bois nor bugles of Vincennes,
nor accordions, bars, or the elegance of ugly women
can hold me back, for I hear sirens –

sirens of factories and ships
and I will go to Manchester:
it will be charming and provincial
I will taste the rustic dishes
I will take my ease amid the clean
Victorian buildings and quiet oils of its canals.

The Embarkation

Hoarded tears
and a sigh on the green surface of a drink.
We were nearly Vikings in our coldness,
our drunkenness and the tendency to rush down on things,
all at once, as if each new idea were a wealthy village
lying undefended on a bay.

The papers had been written,
the texts analysed like tribes
in anthropology. We agreed
it was time to embark.

How the station echoed!
The simplest farewell became Wagner.
The walls of the restaurant were covered
with enormous, pale paintings,
allegorical and so vague
I remember nothing but the colours –
pinks, greys and blues that seemed
to fade even as you looked –
but surely they must have represented
scenes of heroic science and labour,
the building of a new society of steel and glass.

Our actions were unconsidered.
Our thoughts grew like mint.

Somewhere in a sea of tables a voice detached itself:
"...be thankful the religious phase is over.
The old, bearded concepts have been sent into exile –
a permanent one I hope – and we are safe
from their efforts to redeem us. If the moon rose
or rain fell on the theatre terrace
there might be a song...
What was it I wrote once about pigeons?
Now he calls them *flying rats*,
and they are here in multitudes,
a rabble smearing the statues.

My life has not ended. Merely,
it grows a little tired of me."

But anticipation
is always an ample and empty chamber
that exists for you alone to fill, if you wish,
with voices and illuminated scenes,
amid which appear, dimly at first like
dusty windows, the faces of persons
impossibly far removed from you in terms
of handsomeness or wealth, poverty or brilliance.

They are to be desired only in the abstract.
A dry perspective stays fixed.
The mansion or monastery with its graceful stones
is built at another time,
and certain possibilities are ignored
like the possibility of failure in love.

The pause reaches massive proportions –
a kind of coliseum or unused racetrack.

The hope of a good destination is suspended
about you like a vine pierced by sunlight,
but you must first descend;
you must wait in line, impatience leashed.
You are almost there –
I mean at the window where you must buy your ticket
if you are ever to escape this clamorous junction.

But this may not be your fate. Your wallet is empty,
and there is nothing to do but return to the hotel
to sleep and dream. And perhaps this is all for the best:

though invisible, untried
your heart already knows those far towns that only drowse and sing;
the structure, whether colonnade or orange grove,
can't be dismantled...

but as you turn back
the air is cold on your hands.

Surface Reversal

It is night and you are inevitably confused,
having travelled underground,

but now you're happy to find yourself
among the illuminated fountains and young trees.

The city is like a ballade
some people are singing on a bridge,

The wind is a hand pulling back sheet after sheet, –
all black silk, – from the cool bed of the river:

no one sleeps there, so we're told,
but somewhere the linen is heaped or folded.

Dim lights show on a barge
moored against the far quay,

and very obviously this is not a boat
but someone's memory of their lover who died.

The river flows to the west, the wind pulls to the east.
The cathedral dips its fan in both.

The Sudden Ending of Their Dream

The sudden ending of their dream
came when the wall collapsed
and they saw the water-wheel stop turning.
Something like a dust-cloud, but hunched
like an animal, rushed towards them.
They could no longer hear their neighbour
at his piano, and the birds
seemed to drop like stones. So they began again
outfacing what menaced their association.
Whose business was it but theirs? Not
history's or time's. The police were not watching them
although their vans rushed past hissing in the rain,
and black princesses sheltered nervously in doorways.

They began again, –
under the chestnuts in flower, on the bridges,
under the marvellous clouds, beside the statues.
If anything could be saved they would save it.
If life was empty they would bring food and flowers,
wine and illustrated books.
They staggered home in the evenings
carrying bread and enormous newspapers,
still thinking of the bronze head
they had seen in the museum. Light flashed
from the rim of a lunette. Storms of laughter passed over them
A party was always going on in the courtyard below,
and as the wall began to crack behind them
they studied the plans for the kiosk they would build.
It was the old urge not to be shut out of heaven,
not to shut heaven out. The sky kissed their hands.

The Sky My Husband

The sky my husband
The sky my wife
The sky my country and my grief
The sky my courtyard and my fountain
The sky my hyacinth
The sky my flock of birds and my guitar
The sky my kitchen and my knives
The sky my winter coat my summer shirt
The sky my balloon my acrobat
The sky my dancing-floor
The sky my café and my cinema
The sky my park and my path between the statues
The sky my garden of white trees
The sky my carousel
The sky my opera and my madrigal
The sky my actors and my theatre
The sky my wind-mill
The sky my evenings and my books
The sky my taxi my *tabac*
The sky my attic my hotel
The sky my railways and my stations
The sky my cities and my stones
The sky my head my hair my limbs
The sky my eyes my spectacles
The sky my nights my neon
The sky my balcony my garland and my mask
The sky my terrace and my tables
The sky my avenues and bridges
The sky my chandelier my Chinese lantern
The sky my roots and branches
The sky my awnings and my hope
The sky my gulfs my lakes my canyons
The sky my arches and my aqueducts in ruins
The sky my waning moon my child
The sky my rivers and cascades
The sky my forests and my solitude

The sky my castle and my flight of stairs
The sky my windows and my roofs
The sky my aerials and factory chimneys
The sky my pavilion and my tomb
The sky my incense and my hymn
The sky my journals and my magazines
The sky my violin my piano
The sky my medals and my coins
The sky my puddles and my dust
Le ciel mes feux d'artifice
The sky my scarves my hats my gloves
The sky my showers my snow my salt my sleet
The sky my mansions and my mother
The sky my diary and my photographs
The sky my cedars and my roses
The sky my face my cake of soap
The sky my memory my mountains
The sky my paper boat my autumns and my loss
The sky my palms and my Sahara
The sky my porches and my atriums
The sky my galleries my icons
The sky my radio my satellite my video
The sky my drought my famine
The sky my street-lamps my alleys and my crowds
The sky my armies and my guns my death
The sky my exile and my winters
The sky my victories and massacres
The sky my ministries my lies my parliament my eloquence
The sky my labyrinth my irony
The sky my carnation my buttonhole my bed
The sky my rondos and my boredom
The sky my flotillas and my rafts of flowers
The sky my love-affairs my comedies
The sky my theories and forgetfulness
The sky my Paris my New York my Rome
The sky great wheel of lights and colours
The sky my Venice my Vienna and my Petersburg
The sky my Alexandria

The sky my empire my provinces my people
The sky my islands and my harbours
The sky my lullaby
The sky my blood my breath my home
The sky my end

From a High Place

Dear, don't visit me,
or visit me differently like an evening
with descending birds and the speech of bells,
bring with you the echoes of things
happening far away or long ago
like a party in a chateau; let it all
come down at last to mists
and stars like diamonds, to beds
like banks of moss and ferns; let us
lie in the substance of sleep.

The birds fall out of heaven, as sleep does,
and some must die unvisited.
But in the light of the chateau the singers
do not die, but merely change their substance:
they become a print or tape you can repeat
at will. So evening is a blood-orange
or, in the French, it is a storm of blood.

The storms that visit sleep
only loosen the echoes of stars and blood,
of ferns and diamonds,
shaking them free like the repeating notes
of a piano in a prelude by Debussy.
What happens is inevitable we suppose,
though lacking substance, is inevitable
like the print of rain at evening,
or the growth of moss over
an amphitheatre's steps.

These are steps we will descend in sleep
like echoes of ourselves, each singing
in our different ways, without dull repetition,
since that is something very far from our idea
of heaven or understanding or song,
since that is a big sleep, a little death.
I will not be party to this happening, or the lies
spoken in marvellously illuminated chateaux.

Our speech echoes about us
as if each stood in an amphitheatre
alone. We are the prelude to something
beyond our understanding, the tape that winds
on until it leads into an evening
of inevitable change and blood,
under the death-knell of the wind's bell.

It will make echoes of things far away,
which I love but cannot understand, –
things long gone like dead birds
or the idea of heaven repeated on a piano
in the French of Debussy, in the language
of diamonds and mist. Dearest,

alone and singing in the light of a chateau,
in the embrace of an amphitheatre,
visit me not, or differently, –
in a storm of bells, of ferns and petals,
in a rain of oranges and blood,
in the unravelling of this tape in which
what is far from us becomes the substance of our speech.

Dear. Bells. Visit. Echoes. Sleep.
Repeat me now on your piano long ago.

Little Variations for Natalia Ginzburg

Perhaps she had given up hope
of ever seeing the house, the bridge, the moon
even before the thought occurred
that these might be what the distance
sequestered in its silver. There was a mystery
she could solve, a truth whose contours
were both suggested and concealed by the wind
blowing against her face, bearing a vast cool fragrance.

She looked for hours at the moon
but the house did not appear, nor the bridge
and she brushed away her thoughts like moths.
It was her hope to become absolutely clear,
more clear, more distant than the river
at its source. She would not say the light was silver,
although it was, – as near as it had ever been.
She did not want strange fragrances or mysteries
but the sound of human speech on the wind, –
a man, a woman and a child. Ah, hopes,

and distances you draw thought on
like a fragrance filling each room of the furthest house
and, as leaves are carried on the surface of a river,
under the moon, beneath the arches of a bridge,
she found three names were floating in her thoughts, –
those of a man, a woman and a child:
she wrote and every word was minted silver.

The Hotel Brown Poems

1

Above every seaward-facing window
of the Hotel Brown is a canopy. At night
the perfumes of the garden will delight you...

It is a good place to fall in love
and a good place to write, though neither
is obligatory. You must, however,

praise the light, the changing colours
of the sea at dawn and dusk: these are
the divinities of the place. Amen.

2

Once in the cool, blue restaurant
of the Hotel Brown a friend said to me, –
"You don't realise how much your openness
frightens people: it hits them like a wave,"

and I smiled, not because his words
amused me, but because the scent of peppers
grilling in the kitchen overwhelmed me.
I could not think of ideas or people then –

only of the place, the scent, the way
long white curtain moved back and forth
across the boundaries of light and air.

3

The windows were open on to the small terrace.
the sea was motionless. Not a wave. I would not,
for the world, compare it to anything.

I pointed down the half-deserted quay
drowsy with a heat that seemed personal
like a memory, and said, "That man, hunched

as if he were struggling against
a cold wind, is a poet, a friend of mine.
let's make ourselves known."

4

Think of yourself as a wave. Hard.
Think of yourself as open. Equally hard.
Usually your gestures seem to take place
behind a glass partition, fogged with steam

and there is often the sense that things are closing in, –
have closed over you like the waters of a lamentation,
and the absence of obvious locks or bars only confirms
that depressingly, the fault lies in your soul as much

as hostile circumstances, the invisible clouds
of general despondency that hang off even the most
blissful shore, waiting to blow in, dulling
the water, the boats, your deepest words with dust.

5

As we walked towards the temple
the poet said to us: "This may seem
a small island to you but once it was
an independent state with its own fierce navy.

The Athenians destroyed it utterly."
The old ramparts were massive, finely jointed
but the area of jumbled stones and bushes they enclosed
seemed no bigger than a modest public park.

6

We saw him to the evening boat. A man
who walked like a dancer followed him aboard
carrying a single bicycle wheel, and the ship
departed, illuminated, unreasonably festive.

We walked back past the bars. The night
was already richly dark, full of murmured conversation.
Light poured down the steps of the Hotel Brown,
traversed by a cold, rising breeze, as if to say –

"You are welcome, for the moment. This
is an interval in your life. Soon you must look to
the plots and masks and backdrops of your next act.
Here all moments are intervals. It is like music and like loss."

Unsentimental Journey

We see the envelope they are
but the soul of things stays shut
like a library on Sundays.

This is a remote provincial city
in a country you are visiting
for the first time. Who could believe
the depth of the dust covering the trees,
the numbers of burial mounds on the outskirts,
the hamburger joints punctuating the ancient streets?

The more precise the investigation,
the more the 'unknown quantities' multiply,
but it isn't the number of books
or paintings that exist in the world
of which we wished to be assured,
but their quality and veracity, –

the quality also of private impressions,
sudden recalls, customs and performances,
whether these should be set down in one form
or another, or allowed to decay
like towers of unbaked brick.

The rigour you may once have desired
is ruled out, for the objects are
attentive as the dogs in fables,
Ulysses' dog he had to kill, –

and an iridescence like the oil
spilt from gardening machinery
along cemetery walks after the rain
covers the remembered faces:
a good effect, but a puzzling one...

So much wants to exist, –
the echoing station you departed from,
the sandwich wrappers on the train,

the narrow hotel room with its view
of an open-air cinema's blank screen,
besides all the cities of Europe and America...

and when, in a very distant place,
a raised hand releases pennants of blood
you must orchestrate the outcry.

You have suddenly moved in from the margins,
and though you can't say how,
your response will be decisive like a battle
changing the allegiance and religion of a people.

But the most violent actions, the black howls
leave no trace, only an open field
with ruts and hillocks, a fence of trees.

October in the Capital

It was raining in the capital. JOHN ASHBERY

There were rumours or rumbles of rain in the mountains
marking the northern border, but elsewhere
the land remained as if blighted, –

an awning hanging limply in the windless air,
parched and cracked by the continuing drought, –

a place in which bleached arcades
pasted with political slogans dwindled
into formlessness and could not be retrieved:

mostly it seemed a sponge the city
irrigated by its inventions,
but now it was drying out, –
a tray of tobacco leaves
for an industrial tyrant's cigar.

Reports came in of disturbances, –
costumed statues mobbed in the streets,
harmless crones immured in dying wells,

but in the capital lethargy reigned,
as after prolonged bouts of sexual indulgence.
The summer lull,
when everyone and their accountants
vanished from the earth, became deep torpor,
a crevice closing like a sweating fist;
pigeons sat listlessly in squares
waiting for patrons who had fled; people
remained draped over balconies like laundry.

Many thought the world could end like this,
and the moon, glowing more brightly than ever
like an image on a screen, brought no relief
but seemed to burn far beyond the ordinary heat
of day as if it were white metal.

It was the end of October
in the capital. A bus
backfired in the street. A car
crowded with a family
set out for hills where at least
there were canopies of shade
and recent memories of water
in dry streambeds. Arguments
arose operatically in
sweltering tenements
and died into indifference.
Even the noise in restaurants
at weekends lacked *brio*:
the waiters' shouted orders
hung in the air like
weathered shop-signs.

★

One night in the capital
a girl was returning from a party alone,
a little depressed, having failed to speak
to a man who had long fascinated her.
Crossing one of the four bridges that led from the hub
of the city towards the vagueness of the northern suburbs
she stopped before the statue of a handsome, muscular man
in (about) his thirties. Now that she was free
from the press of people and their words
she admired him frankly, and a space opened
in which he, or the thought of his living model,
belonged to her like solitary laughter.
The bridge was deserted and she spoke aloud:

"If you could speak I wonder what you'd say?
You've been here so long, it wouldn't be anything
very cheerful, I suppose. You've seen the traffic change.
Are you sad the horses have gone? They were noble.
They would have suited you. An army has passed

with tanks, and cars for weddings and funerals.
Not far away an old woman sells flowers, –
gardenias a specialty for lovers in the evening.
And there's a newspaper stand. You can read, of course,
and our ways won't impress you but you wouldn't
condemn us. Gods of your kind weren't so
moralistic. Once you must have lived on a mountain
or a cloud. I can't imagine that. Weren't you bored?"

Then the image of a wave occurred to her, –
completely transparent, rising very slowly.
She paused and thought: "What has happened to the air?"
There seemed to be a mist over the river
and a dry rustling began in the oleander leaves,
as if the leaves at last were shaking themselves free
of all the summer's dust, and many heard it
throughout the stifled city. For some it began
as a dream from which they awoke startled and gasping
as if they had been drowning. Many, out of pure animism,
thanked God, thinking the rain *was* God. Others
rushed to hold their faces up into the downpour.
Exhausted dancers leaving clubs revived,
and those who had left early for work paused
in the brief delusion that the wet and shining streets
led somewhere other than a place of labour.

*

It was raining in the capital.
The girl remained where she was, overcome
by a sense of foreboding that became fixed –
a statue made of very cold water.

70

Romanza

for Rosanne Wassermann

Some days the whole of living
is like a phrase you overheard in the subway,
and didn't quite believe, –
it was too eloquent and muddled,
and some more urgent business occupied
your thoughts, as a crowd occupies a square.

The vanished monuments
of Europe edge the square,

and an alien nostalgia
for the banks of the Vistula,
for the steep roofs and stiff pines
of extinct principalities,
and women beating washing at a jetty
recurs like a concerto on the radio.

The last note is immediately present in the first.
The vivid faces of dead families appear,
streaked with photographic rain,
and like late sunlight the clouded voice emerges:

"After so many years,
so many journeys I did not want to take
I still know how to play the violin
in the old style,
humanist, figurative.

A woman breathes in my adagios.
In my allegrettos, mother, or someone like her,
leans over the bed. The pillow is soft,
embroidered with some peaceable motto.

Her bound hair
is a lost cloud architecture
through which the sun
rises in every rondo, shines

on the few children playing,
the few gulls wheeling,
the few boats rocking

beside, above, upon
the flat, remembered sea
at sunset a century ago."

The Banks of the Ohio

The buses would come sometimes three times a week, sometimes twice depending on the weather. They would leave Lubnava-Serbiny, the nearest town of any consequence, very early in the morning and make their way slowly along the valley of the interminable River Sorb, before heading up into the mountains. The passes were formidable, their roadsides punctuated with makeshift crucifixes commemorating travellers who had succumbed to landslides, blizzards or unskilled drivers. The buses were battered, ingrained with dirt. We could hear their brakes screaming some miles away as they approached late in the evening.

It was not to be expected that persons of any distinction would alight at our village. Ours was one of the remotest corners of the Empire, – the butt of many jokes concerning ignorance and bad weather. The few tourists who sometimes found themselves marooned among us looked about with obvious amazement that they could have landed in a place so devoid of interest, without a castle or a mansion, with a church hardly distinguishable from a barn. Though surrounded by crags and forests we had never learnt to be picturesque. We were an obstinate, practical people whose festivals were few. But each year a man would arrive who seemed to justify the existence of the village, seemed to take it into the embrace of the great world beyond the mountains.

He would usually arrive at the beginning of autumn when the first violent winds came down from the passes to denude the trees. It was a time of regret, a time when longings rose up amidst us like mansions of clouds or leaves. And we, – I mean the young people of the village – would listen for the screaming of the brakes. No distant hunting horn ever sounded more melancholy or full of promise as the sound echoed and approached, echoed and retreated. Then the bus would swerve to a stop in a puddle. Geese would waddle off in a panic. Then *he* would alight! I mean *The Traveller*. Then we would see the marvellous suitcase lowered from the steps of the bus, emblazoned with the labels of Nice and New York, Cairo, Stamboul, Buffalo, Bangkok, Paris and Manchester. We had little knowledge of these places and yet the vivid patchwork of the suitcase expressed them all to us. We walked along the broad avenues of these cities; we visited their museums, parks and restaurants; we encountered their most notable citizens and resided for weeks in their most expensive hotels. In truth, of course, very few of us had been further than Nysh, our dismal provincial capital, which history had largely neglected since an efficient Turkish massacre in the sixteenth century.

As soon as he alighted we would gather around him full of questions:

"Are the fogs of London as beautiful as they say?

Is it true that the Holymen of India can remove their eyes from their sockets and still see more clearly than you or I?

In Burma aren't there cities of pagodas infested with vultures?

Do the women of Russia dress entirely in furs and jewels rescued from the bellies of fish?

Isn't it true that in France in the Spring the young women dance on the bridges while the young men sing to them from boats moored beneath?

Don't persons in Egypt dwell in the tombs of their ancestors?

In China, I hear that the people are averse to all forms of direct statement.

In certain islands of the Indonesian archipelago a person is shunned if he or she is not at all times graceful.

In parts of Africa aren't ebony masks of family members buried beneath hearthstones?

In Japan it is the custom, is it not, for newly-weds to leap from waterfalls?

In America the automobiles are as large as yachts.

Are all Eskimos tattooed?"

Sometimes he would make some evasive, tantalizing reply, but more often he would merely shake his head and walk off in the direction of the inn. There he would stay for two months or three. He would rarely go out, or if he did so it was at a time when no one saw him. We never discovered why he came. It was thought that he came to relax, to escape from the wonders and anxieties of the great world, and perhaps to work at some personal project, – an account of his travels for example. He would not talk about his experiences which remained as mysterious to us as the life of the distant capital. He would not answer idle questions but if someone should approach him in need of advice or information concerning something vital to their existence

74

his response was always sober and generous. There might some-times be irony in his narrow smile, but never condescension. His learning amazed us but his manner was never boastful or arrogant and his advice was always found to be good. He was regarded with great respect, as a man of knowledge who had chosen to come among us, and yet after a time a certain resentment would begin to show itself, shadowing almost imperceptibly the unvary-ing courtesy with which he was treated. What was his purpose? What was his interest in our lives? He seemed to be observing us from a great distance. Gossips would remark that he drank more brandy than was wise and rose too late in the day. He would always leave before this resentment became open hostility. It was the crowning courtesy.

Many theories and suppositions surrounded him: he was a philosopher, a poet, a scientist, a disillusioned priest, the youngest son of an aristocratic family, or only a man who had failed in love. But a maid who, in a moment of forgetfulness, entered his room without knocking obstinately claimed he was a photographer. She found him, apparently hard at work, kneel-ing on the floor and so absorbed that he did not at first notice her. The table, the bed, the walls and most of the floor of the room were covered with photographs of cities, geographies and peoples that obviously could not exist, for the people had many eyes and were winged, and the buildings (which seemed to defy the laws of gravity) surpassed in size and grandeur the great monuments of the capital: there were suspended buildings and spherical buildings; there were buildings balanced on a point like inverted pyramids and pencil-thin towers enmeshed in winding ramps and elevated causeways. Her accounts were confused and contradictory. She had only glimpsed the pictures for a moment and many of them were indistinct, out-of-focus as if taken in great haste. She was a simple girl and many people doubted her word. True, there weren't many books in the village, but she might have seen books of fairy-stories or an illustrated Bible, since the winged people sounded very like cherubim or seraphim, yet she remained tearfully insistent that she had seen what she had seen, that the pictures were not drawings or paintings, that she had not "made it up." Furthermore there is no doubt that she had been greatly alarmed by what she saw. The Traveller, for his part, seems to have been more horrified and embarrassed than angry at her intrusion. He looked at her and she ran, – along the corridor and down the stairs until she came to rest on a bench before the inn where the proprietress comforted her.

Her reports were discussed for many years, – years in which he did not appear – and inevitably distortion and exaggeration did their work. What else could account for the floating city inhabited by giant cats, the forest of sprouting oblongs, the intelligent fire, or the Emperor of the glass garden? These were not images of our present time, however distant they might be in space. They were the images of his absence or of marvels the world did not contain.

Some five years later he returned, and we saw that he was old. The suitcase was horribly scarred, many of its labels obliterated, and there were no new ones that we could see. I remember my mother saying that now he had come to die. "But why here," I asked, "where he is admired but knows nobody?" She could not answer but held to her opinion. It was the beginning of winter. The next day he appeared in hiking clothes and announced that he wished to visit an old monastery located two days journey south of the village, in the direction of Varna. He wanted to know whether its frescoes really were as fine as certain intrepid nineteenth-century travellers had reported. We assured him that the frescoes had been badly damaged by gunfire in the civil wars, and that the inclement winters of recent years would surely have obliterated what remained. We further warned him of the dangers of such an expedition at that time of year. But he was obstinate. His face closed and he shouldered his pack. There was no farewell committee, – such a thing would have embarrassed him – but as he left the village many people appeared at their doors and windows. As he passed out of sight snow began to fall. We did not see him turn round, but perhaps he looked back towards us from beyond that veil, and perhaps he thought of us with some affection. We did not see him again. After a month had passed the proprietress of the inn summoned the courage to open the suitcase but found that it contained nothing but an alarm-clock and a dictionary. And soon we forgot about him. The times were difficult. Buses came only once a week. Violent changes came from which our remoteness did not protect us, and soon we all had to travel, – not in order to discover the wonders of the world, but in order to escape destruction. This is what I will always regret, that my travelling was forced. What I had dreamed of so many times brought only terror and fatigue, and everywhere I felt I was in the same place: each place was an ignorant village with its priests, its mothers and its tyrants.

I have come to rest at last, – if "rest" is the term – in a one-bedroom apartment, twenty stories up in a high-rise by the muddy Ohio River. As I write helicopters circle above the disorderly crowds swarming at the riverfront. They are protesting the recent killings. There can be no end to this though forty years have passed.

View through the Glass Door

Don't waken the lamp. Don't drive out the twilight, –
the wind and the rain would laugh
at its patched, grey coat.

It comes to remind us of something, –
a pattern of flowers, a transparent distance that has
no brothers or sisters in the damp gardens of these suburbs.

The hospital beds recede like steps
leading to a winter lake.

Nothing can alter
the imperfection in your eye.

Prepare the table in the next room.
Place bread on the cloth.
Turn the radio down. Sweep dust

from the hallway, wipe the mirror
and wait with hands folded.

Leaves have covered the doorstep, inches deep.
The car horn answers itself from the boarded windows.

Part III: Interlude

Low-Flying Aircraft: An Eclogue

AMYNTAS
STREPHON
EUNICE, *a lady from Harlem*

Scene 1

AMYNTAS:

How unnerving the country is today!
It's too elaborate,

STREPHON:

and sad.

AMYNTAS:

But *con fuoco* . . .

STREPHON:

in a late romantic way.

AMYNTAS:

These clouds are too fast for me.
At home they seem to keep their place,
Like flags above the buildings,
But here, they confuse me more
Than the wildest intersection
As they roll over the twisting valleys
Of slow rivers, those rivers
With names like the speech of primitives
Frightened by a loathsome God.

AMYNTAS & STREPHON:

O Unk, Usk, Onney, Clun, Lugg and Wye!

STREPHON:

I must confess I too prefer
A taxi's soothing purr.

The gold pouring down on the meadow,
Burning my hands, is a shadow
Compared to the light of a rainy street –
And routes of adventures
Departing from my feet!...

Besides, to measure time according to the reports
Of bird-scarers in a house facing
The wrong way...

AMYNTAS:

For *what*?

STREPHON:

                Or even
To ride past fields of flowering peas
And blue lucerne does not make one wiser
Or the world saner.

AMYNTAS:

         Indeed not! Nor trees
Whose gestures are disclaimers,
And do not trust the flowers,
But greet them with glowers.

EUNICE:

Doesn't this just remind you
Of the beautiful Hudson?

AMYNTAS & STREPHON:

No! Onk, Unney, Ledrake and Glugg!

Scene 2

STREPHON:

My dear, I recall the dawn of our careers
When we travelled sweetly with our fathers

Gathering string along the hedgerows,
But everything has changed...

AMYNTAS:

And must change.

STREPHON:

    Alas and cheers!
This ale is nauseous.

AMYNTAS:

    Don't mope.
A huge bookshop full of dust
Has landed in the small town
Asleep beside its river
And is at once the focus of all hope –
Like a spaceship bringing benign
And wonderfully intelligent monsters.

STREPHON:

That dust is gold dust!
The sneezing is a celebration!
The rush begins, severally...

AMYNTAS:

The river is flowing past the windows!

STREPHON:

The windows of the bookshop and all
The windows of the mud-built town!

AMYNTAS:

But despite the assurance like a smile
Of this unchanging mutability –
The events exploding with a certain style
There remain questions we could ask
Forever. Is it, after all, *a river*?
Shouldn't one call it a blue lassoo?

And isn't *that* like an arm
With a sentimental tattoo...?

STREPHON:

Yes, and this is like the delicate shell of a nautilus...
O, it *is* the delicate shell of a nautilus. I see.

AMYNTAS & STREPHON:

Uh. Umm. Uhuh. Ummmmmm.

EUNICE:

Honey, those slashed meadows of print
Are useless for pillows. Don't buy them.

Scene 3

STREPHON:

The night took so long on its way
Why weren't we warned about the delay?

AMYNTAS:

The dark trees sigh, and a moth beats its wings.
You won't sleep much under a roof that sings.

STREPHON:

Aren't you Prince O, and this whole landscape
The quilts you have heaped up in your despair
For your night alone in the dismal boat
Under hanging trees that remind you, as trees do...

AMYNTAS:

As flowers will,

STREPHON:

of she who,

AMYNTAS:

> or he who

STREPHON:

> is not there.

EUNICE:

The sun goes down slowly
As if sunset were somethin' holy.
No one goes dancin' here,
How far away is Harlem Mere.
The absence of excitin' men
Leaves me lonely as a chatelaine,
Stitching a veil to the end of crusades.
My poor heart bumps down
The moon's long glissades.
O night goin' down
In the crevice of a frown, –
No one goes dancin' here,
How far away is Harlem Mere...*etc*

Scene 4

AMYNTAS:

There is an arrow of water in my heart!

STREPHON:

Is this a mood the land imparts?

AMYNTAS:

I don't know. I think the drapes and gauzes
Falling raggedly in haunted loops
Over this bucolic scene of oaks and vanished abbeys
Where, by mistranslation, a valley is made 'golden'
Are my own invention.

STREPHON:

Perhaps so,
But leaving aside dissatisfaction's foil,
And letting the silly sheep wander as they may
Over the mounds of heroes and raving serfs,
Isn't there something in this view
We might imitate, something both
Intimate and spacious like a palace
With well-appointed rooms for sulking in,
Grand staircases and bathrooms? A generosity...

AMYNTAS:

Perhaps the mood invents the landscape,
So the moon is always the wasted moon
Of a narrow attic window, or else it is full
And suave like the horn in the dead Infanta's
Pavane; then clouds and stars strike gongs and bells,
And the prince is in his pagoda. The scene shifts...

EUNICE:

Are these the locals honey?
They sure talk funny,
But it's quite the nicest
Sound I've heard
From Pisa to Peru,
And every one of them's
As pretty as a bird!

AMYNTAS & STREPHON:

Lady, we thank you
For your wisdom.

EUNICE:

Kids, you're welcome!

Part IV

A Long Encounter
for Maggie Paley

Only the dead don't know
what heaven's like. For the rest
extrapolation is possible.

To meet someone for the first time
and immediately adore them, as if
they were the sun, would be one instance.

I don't mean you should fall in love
with this person, simply that when they speak
from the far side of a littered table

you should know you have entered a new country,
and its landscape, architecture and songs
will continue to embrace and fascinate you

through long years. An avenue has opened
and its trees are pricked with lights.
There is nothing you can't afford, if what

is expended is sympathy. These people
are to be treasured and celebrated
as if each were a public holiday, –

the planting of a first harvest
after a long and terrible voyage,
the construction of the first house in a wilderness.

The Men

The men in the next building sound so damn cheerful
you'd think they were drunk or had won the lottery.

The yellow locust leaves tremble with apprehension –
how big everything seems all of a sudden.

The men are smashing things up, they are ripping things out –
they are nearly dancing on the old boards, the old bricks and
    windows.

Evicted families of objects huddle on the sidewalk
trying not to think about the winter that is coming.

And the men go to it like whalers.
What does it matter how much intelligence there was in the beast?
One of them emerges grinning with a tortured piece of plumbing;
its cries can be heard the length of the block.
Remorse is as foreign to them as Vienna.

They appear to be filling the back of a beat-up truck
with an asphyxiating hill of dust,
and the same dust is spreading across my floor
as if I'd spilt something, a bottle of grey milk perhaps?

They don't stop. Their bellowed jokes
fly through the air like arrows in a Japanese battle-scene.
I think they are renovating an apartment,
they are 'making it new,' and certainly I should applaud,
but on days like today when it's beginning to rain
I'd rather leave things to crumble as they may.
Think of the whole city
sinking in on itself like a wooden coffin!
It would be a grand decay, almost Roman...

They wouldn't think so,
and it's not that they're paid to think differently, –
optimism's legitimate offspring, they really don't agree.
I don't insist. I think a compromise could be reached. Do they?

The Turquoise Steps

During the long hours of the afternoon
the sun sat on the turquoise steps, –

his shoulders drooping until
the songs in the street revived him.

But he feared an early death and began
to fidget about the rooftops and cornices

looking for a way out. A woman
climbed to the door with difficulty,

wheezing: for her the turquoise steps
went on forever. And the bells would not sound.

The steps led only to the door
and a narrow grey corridor,

but everything could be reversed: the steps
led down into the wide world

and in their colour and form contained
the idea of a woman in a marvellous dress,

descending effortlessly toward a blue lake,
calm and mild in the evening light,

and her dress was the light in which she would return
again and again without boredom,

holding her white flowers
and a crumpled message of forgiveness.

The Great Tower of Samaria

It was a soporific evening in early September. I was walking up Avenue X, when I came to an empty block surrounded by fencing. A series of billboards proclaimed: WORLD'S TALLEST BUILDING, SOON TO BE COMPLETED. I slowed my pace and, finding a broad gap in the fence, peered through. I couldn't see much. All I could make out was a huge, dim excavation. I was not even sure I could see to the bottom of it, the street lights were so weak and widely spaced.

It was at this point that I felt something prod me in the back. A nervous voice said: "I've got a knife. Don't look round. Hand over your wallet and you won't get hurt." The words seemed formal and rehearsed like obsolete courtesies. It was as if I had been expecting this all along. I felt that this was happening to someone else, and that the real "I" was watching it all from a safe distance. Nonetheless, I knew enough not to argue, and without checking to see if there was indeed a knife at my back I did as I was told. But the transaction was not over, and with a sardonic word of thanks, I was pushed through the gap in the fence.

I expected to drop like a stone into the darkness and, perhaps, die (it was out of my hands), but instead found myself sliding down a steep slope of loose earth and rubble. I was unable to stop myself and seemed to fall for some time. As luck had it I landed in a pile of sand or fine gravel, bruised but otherwise unhurt. I must have been dazed for a few moments but eventually I made out that I was standing on a rough, concrete floor from which arose an apparently limitless forest of unfinished pillars.

I considered what I should do. I tried calling out a few times, but the street was a long way above me, and I realized that no sensible person would stop for a voice calling out of the darkness on Avenue X at that hour. I reasoned that there had to be a way out, and began to work my way along the edge of the concrete floor, but, after falling over several piles of metal rods, and, in the process, tearing my clothing and cutting my knees, I decided it was best to stay put. It was, – as I have mentioned – a warm night, and daylight would bring an end to my problems. I sat down with my back against a pillar and very soon fell asleep.

When I awoke I found myself in a small room lit by a single

fluorescent tube. The room contained nothing but a pair of battered filing cabinets, both of them thick with dust. (The odd thing, I now realize, is that none of this seemed unusual: I might have been waking in my own bedroom with nothing more urgent on my mind than the thought that the ceiling needed painting.) The room had a door, of course, and I opened it. I stepped out into a wide corridor. It seemed to be part of a little-used basement or sub-basement and I could hear the sound of people typing in the distance. A flight of stairs at the far end of the corridor suggested that I would have no difficulty in finding my way to street level, so I climbed the stairs briskly, only to emerge into a small but well-appointed lobby with fig-trees and leather-clad chairs. There was no one about and no apparent access to the street, so I climbed another flight of stairs and arrived at a similar but larger and more elegantly decorated lobby, with fashionable journals scattered on a low table surrounded by another artistic grouping of chairs. One wall was occupied by an original "oil" resembling the water-lilies of Monet. And so it went on. The third lobby was all golden curlicues, mirrors, allegories and urns in niches. The fourth favoured heavy drapes and potted palms. In one corner was a piano, a copy of Schumann's *Dichterliebe* lying open upon it.

In none of these rooms were there people, – which is why I hurried on. And yet every room I entered, every level to which I ascended seemed to have been abandoned, just at that moment, by a busy crowd, – a crowd (perhaps) of architects, builders, labourers, decorators, technicians, cleaning women, secretaries, artists, financiers, executives, and besides these, all manner of persons bearing petitions, applications, complaints, or proposals. Often I thought that I caught an echo of retreating footsteps and conversations as if gongs and violins were dying at the end of a symphony.

On the fifth level I found myself in a hall of some magnificence. Its walls were lined with a dark, reddish marble but for one wall which was covered entirely by a mural representing *The Rape of Europa*. This detained me for some time. Somehow one gained the impression that this Europa was getting the better of the God in his unconvincing bull-disguise. On the same level I discovered an elevator. Its massive doors parted with a faint chime and I entered. At once it began to ascend. I looked for some indication of the floor-level, but there was only one word and one number on the door: ASCEND and 179.

From its slight, shuddering motion, and a faint, eerie, whistling sound I knew the elevator was ascending at great speed. Things remained like this for some minutes, when, suddenly the number 179 glowed red, and the doors parted. I stepped into a wide columned hall some three stories high. There were slender octagonal pillars, lines of small trees in ponderous brass pots, and a fountain. The whole resembled a cross between a hypostyle hall and a Persian *apadana*. A long way off there were doors and windows. I hurried in their direction, becoming more and more puzzled as I did so. Wasn't I on the 179th floor? But weren't there quite ordinary buildings beyond the doors where there should have been nothing but thin air?

I pushed through the doors to discover that Avenue X lay only a short flight of steps below me. A crowd filled the avenue. At the sight of me they let out a roar of acclamation. Liveried flunkies approached from either side and urged me towards a temporary podium at the top of the steps. A man I recognized as the city's mayor swept up to me and shook me warmly by the hand: "Very proud occasion," he muttered, "most auspicious..." Since I seemed to have no choice in the matter I ascended the podium and coughed into the microphone. A murmur of appreciation passed through the crowd as if I had said something apt and witty. I forced a smile, opened my mouth, and closed it again. In the end all I could think to say was: "Hello everyone, I've been robbed." This was not what the crowd wanted to hear. There was an angry rumble, a few shouts, and a general surge forward. The flunkies showed signs of panic and began to tear at their wigs. The mayor dodged backwards with surprising agility. I also stepped back and fell. I must have struck my head. When I came to I was in the position in which I had fallen asleep. A brawny foreman was standing over me saying: "This is private property. You're trespassing. There'll be a fine to pay." I responded somewhat stiffly: "I did not choose to be here," to which he replied: "Who does?" I am still fighting the case in the courts. The world's tallest building has almost reached ground level.

The Spigots

The fire-hydrant sprays the passing cars again
and the loud idea of summer rises in the street
as something to be shared like money or a neighborhood.
Sky over the Hudson shifts from blue to rose,

and a sign glitters there like a cheap brooch.
The half-moon that had been hanging all day
while jets turned circle states at last,
in full voice, its simple proposition,

that when the lights die on the skyscrapers
no one on a roof will be able to look
at anything but this singular moon
out of a Chinese or American poem.

Heat's residue makes your feet sink
into tar and graffiti whose white loops
and scrawls may be names or slogans
but weren't meant for your understanding.

Children are laughing outside the grocery store.
It is much too late for them to be awake.
The excited or impassive faces of their mothers
appear from high windows, utter words, retreat.

In the Street

Man has loved nature too much.
It is time to love man. And woman.

And the works of each. We must hurry
While the colours last,

As emptiness and redundancy
Approach head-on like trucks.

Destruction follows from the first premise.
In the sunsets you can see it happening.

In the tired lineaments of buildings
It is written as a fateful paragraph.

If a small plant takes root above
The cornice of the power-station, that is not hope.

Trees, in their way, are astonishing,
Especially on summer evenings,

But all you can do is leave them alone,
Which cannot happen. So the canopy is removed.

Man is an abuse. He writes the history of loathing
On the cracked mirror of the earth.

But the face you might elicit
From a doorway and some windows on the street

Is different: erase its frown,
The wrinkles of its mouth.

Grail Legend

The hurricane has passed,
the tremors are dying out in Westchester county
and the search for the perfect restaurant continues.
So many openings and closures
keep us constantly on the move.
The avenues are long, they have no end;
chefs switch allegiance, bringing disaster
and those who would dine
wander as in a fog lit by pale marsh-fires.

We must thread our way
through a labyrinth of rumours.
We distrust all praise. Our hearts sink
at the prospect of tonight's waiter
with his soliloquy longer than any of Hamlet's,
his perfect complexion, his possible mendacity.

So the chicken tastes of fish
and is returned, alas,
to the enigmas of the kitchen.

If there is a god
he is a Maître d'.

If there is a perfect dish
it has not been found,
(though we imagine it bathed
in sacramental candle-glow,
ambitiously garnished, yet adorable
as a child's bed-time cup of soup).

If the quest is futile
no one will admit it.

The Golden Windows

Who knows what drives us to persist
after a sleepless night, stencilled
with the vivid troubles of someone else's youth,

in the reading of a tedious saga
in which darkness prevails until the eleventh hour,

when the kitchen still waits
to be installed, the phone needs to be
connected, and the golden windows
glimmer dimly, at all times of the day,
on the far side of a filthy airshaft
six stories high? So today

a boy brought you a purple iris
and it lives in a bottle. How
did it get itself, how do I get myself
into this peculiar situation –
like suddenly waking on the streets
of a foreign city? No doubt –

"a wink and it is gone"
but the eye stays open like the mouth
of a tunnel leading under a river
and the avenues, tall as obelisks,
don't forsake you but fill you with their voices,
and the blue breath of autumn;

and all the windows of the street begin to shimmer
with the syllables of a message you cannot receive.

Move on. Take a hand. Accept this song.

The Monuments

Each year the monuments grew larger.
The citizens demanded this.
As their lives got worse they wanted
longer staircases to descend, towering fountains . . .

Taxes were increased. A famine settled in.
An inexplicable epidemic appeared.
Autumn was rain-sodden. So,
they collected funds for a new work

in the form of a giant, granite pineapple
encircled by a narrow staircase,
so difficult to climb some said
it symbolized life or friendship.

The monuments meant nothing of course.
The misfortune seemed undeserved.
At parties the food was served
on plates in the form of clouds

that descended from the ceiling,
and under each unseasonal strawberry
a gold leaf was set. Despite these strategies
the general melancholy increased.

Poems concerned themselves
with childhood, autumn and failure,
although it was understood that these took the place
of events too unbearable to discuss.

Work resumed on the pineapple.
It was decided to enclose it within a transparent
sphere inscribed with a poem concerning
autumn and failure. Meanwhile

in the downtown area, work began on a new
staircase, some 900 feet high, leading to
a colossal weeping eye. On rainy days
citizens would gather to watch the way

it vanished sweetly into mist,
but no one dared to place a foot
on even the lowest, shining step:
"This is art," they said, "We cannot use it."

The Vase

is a sculpture that will hold flowers.
Bearing the tanned face of a doll
surrounded by burnt sheets of paper,
it is like the funerary monument
of a princely child standing beside
the old highway to China (in

the Tarim Basin perhaps, where
an entire wooden city has crumbled away –
below sea-level, but dry as dust).

Coral dust. Anabasis.

Soon like bunched spears decorated
with the tail-feathers of yellow birds,
forsythia will appear, but you
will remain resolute for autumn
backed by the blue emptiness
that whistles through
the pin-holes of your eyes.

Funeral Preparations in the Provinces

One morning in autumn father died after a long, but not too painful illness. There was no time for expressions of grief. The whole family thought of the work that lay ahead. It was unthinkable that father's funeral should be improperly furnished. Mother was indefatigable, attending to every detail. First they built the two horses and the chariot out of wickerwork. Mother insisted that the horses had to look lively and the chariot must be sturdy. She reasoned that since father had always enjoyed travelling whenever he had the opportunity, now that he had so much leisure time, he would doubtless want to travel the length and breadth of the next world, meeting its famous men, viewing its splendid landscapes. In the chariot they placed certain things he might need on his travels – a water-flask, a satchel with many compartments, a sunhat and a short cape to keep off the rains. A chariot was not the most convenient means of transport, of course, but mother reminded them that they were an old family, and they must think of the great days when their ancestors had been the esteemed advisors of emperors and statesmen.

Secondly, they built the house. It was really a small palace, all in miniature. They included all the furnishings he might need, from tables and chairs to mirrors and candlesticks. The kitchen was amply equipped with jars of herbs, spices and sauces, besides steamers, ladles and shining woks. In the dressing-room they hung his favourite dressing-gowns, his best suits and a tiny, grey fedora. In the study his flute rested on a sideboard, and in the same room was a black grand piano – something he had never possessed in life but had always desired. The library contained all the novels he had ever enjoyed, with pride of place given to *Madame Bovary* and *The Dream of the Red Chamber*. And because she worried that he might get bored during eternity (at least until she joined him) mother also included all the other novels she could think of – the longer the better – complete sets of Balzac, Dickens, Richardson, Stendhal, Tolstoy and Proust. The task of writing the names of authors and novels in gold on the spines of these miniature books (the actual pages of the books were mostly blank) fell to the eldest son. As may be imagined he suffered agonies in the task, and when it was completed his eyes were so red with strain that he looked as if he had been crying for days. And because the house had too many rooms for one man to keep clean and tidy – even if his youth should be returned to him in the afterlife – mother also thought it wise to include servants, two charming girls and a handsome boy. She was determined that their faces should wear expressions of *absolute devotion*. This was very difficult to achieve in such small figures but the youngest son was very good at this kind of thing, and at last everything was completed to her satisfaction. Or so they thought.

By now they had worked for several days, almost without sleeping, but the charming appearance of father's model palace made it all seem worthwhile. It was at this point that mother announced that father had always loved gardening so they must, of course, make a garden for him. This came as something of a surprise to the children since they could only remember their father sitting or strolling in the garden, and that very infrequently. Most of the time he preferred to keep to his study from whence they would often hear the sound of his flute issuing, cool and a little melancholy, in the evenings. But it was impossible to argue with their mother who, besides, was a widow in mourning. They would have been social outcasts if it had become known that they had done so, and since the three daughters had done most of the gardening during father's lifetime – it was they who set about making a garden for him now.

They worked with passion and imagination and when they had finished everyone agreed that they had excelled themselves. There were winding, white-sanded paths (for which they used finely ground sugar), and willows made of wire painted green drooped over pools made of mirror-glass on which paper lotuses were firmly glued, and there were lanterns the colour of jade and pavilions from the eaves of which hung the smallest bells in the world (and these were made from scraps of kitchen foil). Also there were shrines and tinsel waterfalls and chrysanthemums the colour of burnished bronze. The three daughters fairly considered the delights of their garden to be inexhaustible. Even mother had difficulty concealing her pride in her clever daughters – why you'd almost think they were sons! And yet she was a little disappointed that there were no carp in the pools, and perhaps they should have provided at least a brook and a boat since father had always enjoyed rowing on the river (which was so enormous they could not represent it), but she had to admit that there was no time left for these extensions and revisions. It was time to bury father.

It was a blustery, rainy day when they set out with the horses, the chariot, the house, the garden and father's stiff corpse loaded onto a cart and covered with an awning for protection. As they started out the rain set in with renewed force. Even the chrysanthemums wore a defeated air. (I mean the real chrysanthemums in the real, unkempt garden of the real, dilapidated house.) Dark clouds moved swiftly across the sky like torn rags. The old nag that was pulling the overloaded cart seemed, on several occasions, inclined to give up. The cart-wheels stuck fast in mud time and again. When, at last, they reached their destination the whole family was soaked to the skin and exhausted, and mother's umbrella had blown inside out so often that a number of spokes were broken. Looking at the cemetery they almost despaired. How were they to light a pyre with the rain falling so heavily and the ground such an ocean of mud? But Fate smiled on them, for the rain ceased suddenly, the wind dropped, and the kindling, which had been stored beneath the corpse during the journey, was still relatively dry. So they set father on the pile of kindling and around him they disposed the funeral furnishings in ceremonious fashion. After several failed attempts the fire took and, urged on by the autumn wind, soon grew to a small inferno. Mother reached into her fat leather purse and scattered a handful of banknotes into the flames. Now he would want for nothing. They watched for a long time while their days of passionate endeavour rose to the heavens in a dark cloud. They could not think what to say, and at last they wept. They wept for their father who was dead, but they wept much more for the prancing horses, the elegant chariot, the gleaming kitchen, the devoted servants, the piano, the flute, the library of noble books and the garden of a thousand delights.

It came to them at last that something had gone out of the world and would never return to them however much love, imagination and skill they might expend. They saw the end of everything in the black cloud above them, and also they saw the wisdom of their ancestral customs. Only mother remained dry-eyed. When the fire was out and the ashes were interred she fetched a deep sigh and, for a moment, grief descended on the worn features of her face. There was a long silence. At last she shrugged and said: "Well, I don't know if it works, but at least he can't complain. Everything has been done correctly." She further reflected that after so much expense there was no money left for a gravestone – not even the simplest gravestone with the mere name of the dead person written on it. All that would be left was a low mound, and this, she reminded them, had been the fate of many an emperor, so they should not feel embarrassed.

Four Poems After Li Ho

Ballad of Ancient Times

Bright day dies beyond the western mountain
And blue clouds unfurl in the heavens.

So it has always been: a thousand years
Are carried off like dust on the wind.

The sands of the ocean turn to stone. Where once stood
The Bridge of Ch'in bubbles rise from the mouths of fish.

Advancing time knows neither pause nor purpose.
Useless, now, to search for the bronze pillars of Han.

Song: The Peonies

Before lily stems have broken surface, when fragrant grasses lie
    withered,
Rich carriages race to gather rare varieties of bloom.

Water the scented earth in the half-moon-shaped pot.
One night the green chamber breaks open to reveal white daybreak.

At the party in the misty garden a pretty girl pours wine.
Petals of the evening flower are scattered wide, the butterflies also.

The King of Liang grows old in retirement but, for a time, his silk
    robes remain.
On the breeze his long sleeves dance to the tune *The Harp of Shu*.

When the sun wraps itself in veils of cloud, gauze curtains darken.
When a mist of powder falls from a lovely woman's face her lord
    withdraws his love.

Golden boys and golden girls – where have they gone to sleep?
Where the moon shines clear on pavilion and terrace only swallows
    whisper.

Ballad of South Mountain

Transparent autumn wilderness, fresh autumn breeze.
Shrill cries of insects above the deep azure of the pool.

Mists bloom as if rooted in the mossy rocks of the mountains.
As a young girl sheds tears, chill, red petals shed dew.

In September rice-fields are glazed with yellow.
Dim fire-flies slant above the narrow paths.

Spring water breaks from stone and sinks into sand.
Brilliant ghost-lights lacquer the pine-cones.

Ballad of the Old Men and the Blue-Jade Water

They must search for jade only in the purest, blue-jade water.
They must work the jade for a courtesan's swaying aigrette.

The old men are hungry and cold, and the dragon of the waters
    grieves.
The blue water trembles with anger that its purity is sullied.

At night, under the rain they lie on the bare hillside gnawing
    chestnuts.
Blood fills the cuckoo's throat as tears fill the old men's eyes.

The blue water is tired of humankind.
The souls of the drowned cannot forgive the freezing element.

Wind and rain roar through the cypress tree.
Roped together, straining against the current, their feet in the
    stream-bed,

the old men think of a poor village, a simple house, their children
    far away.
Above a ruinous jetty stone steps climb overgrown with grass, –

The grass called "Hanging Intestines" or "Never Forget Me,"
The grass called "Thinking of Home" or "Parting Forever."

The Nine Moons of Austin

1

The grackles and mockingbirds have just fallen silent.
The side of an office tower at sunset is a page of gold.
A cat with a tail like a raccoon's comes to visit.
An abandoned dog howls all night outside a small, fake castle.
The dome of the Capitol is visible through the trees.

2

It's hot by the creek and the water's low.
If it weren't for the fact that some trees are bare
who'd guess it was winter?
Magnolias and live-oaks keep their leaves.

3

Lake Austin is half-drained. It looks wild
but, in this respect, resembles the pools
in the Japanese gardens. The lake-dwellers
have two weeks to repair their wooden docks.

4

A water tower like a ritual mace,
made for smashing skulls, rises from a hillside.
It is so incongruous that everything around it, –
the hills fanning out into blue-drenched distance,
the dwarfish trees, seem strange beyond words.
No human intelligence seems to be involved,
though on all sides dwellings are concealed
in the dry undulations of the land.

5

Odours the sun draws from the earth after a day of rainstorms.
The redbud in bloom: on the divided island,
jacarandas of fifteen years ago.

Onrush of memory:
bordered by white iris, a steep path
leads down to the creek in flood

6

A tribe of bluejays stages a parliament
in the branches of a juniper.
The grackles return, in frenzy,
to the Capitol.

7

We are perhaps five miles away. The city
on its long ridge, seems to rise straight out of a wilderness, –
its towers and domes gracefully disposed, singly or in clusters
at some distance from each other. For a moment
we might be in the Yucatan, and this
a centre for ceremonies we can only guess at
from the evidence of brilliant but mildewed frescoes, –

the men and their victims
dressed like Birds of Paradise.

8

Again the many birds are silenced.
The black dog with one white paw has gone
in search of a new master.
In the green of the bamboo the cardinal
makes his last appearance of the day,
utters a single note, bright as his colour, vanishes.

9

Above the city a long train of
white cloud begins to cross the night sky.
The door is open and the air is warm.
The cat returns to sit unmoving and compact
under the chair in which you write
at the desk supported on empty wine-cases.
You are translating from the German,
difficult words: *heilignüchterne*,
meaning both "holy" and "lucid"
like this moment of stillness and clouds
passing, noble as Hölderlin's swans.

Pianola Music (Double Portrait)

1

I bought a bird-house
but, for a month, no birds seemed to call.
Now they come, but they're only sparrows or grackles...
On certain mornings it's hard not to interpret
like the gloomiest scholar. The sparrows
are students, perhaps, without a thought in their heads
except the ones their adored teacher planted there.
And the grackles? Well, the grackles
with their voices like the sound of crude,
wind-up toys, must be critics of course: they dump
on anything stationary in the parking-lot.

Nothing can be relied upon it seems.
Not the bird-house. Not the house.
Or the love people bear for you,
though they bear it obviously like a floral basket.
It is something you'd like to accept, but where
would you put it? Could it live
as a punctuation at the turn of the stairs
or on the long table in the sun-flooded kitchen?

The light is a base you touch each day,
yet it reflects off any willing surface,
it deflects and diffuses the dark thoughts of separation
night intruded like a claw. Even
your own outline dissolves in this solution,
and the gilded spines of old adventure novels catch fire
with a fire like that of some rural catastrophe
that actually harms no one, –

the crops are all safe and shadows cast by
skyscrapers of flame are made of some gorgeous
purple stuff that unravels over the landscape,
collecting in spoiled heaps at the horizon.

The spectators in the fields like it so much
they join hands and drink to the event.

2

The ordinary blessings are
entered in the journal.

There are windows and doors that open.
There is a veranda for the summer.
There is conversation in the evenings
and the preparation of meals.
There are patriotic tunes,
Episcopalian hymns...
(They'll let you sing anything.)

The street leading down to the river
on which only garages seem to open,
painted hard-to-describe, faded shades of grey and plum
seems a permanent, cool backwater of autumn
where the "Tree of Heaven" drops its leaves.

The courthouse square is beautiful today, –
it is so much how you always wanted it to be,
classically so, shaded by trees, bordered by churches, –
not impervious, but crisp and resistant
to the mill-race of too much randomness.
That's why you petitioned against the new bandstand:
it was already *enough* in the words of the chorale.

So, you have looked at the square,
you have looked at the mountains and the river
(and you have looked at the paintings of these scenes)
you have looked at the woods in autumn
and the houses in the form of Greek temples.

If you still don't know quite what to make of it all,
who would, given so much material for vision
and these things are like you a little, aren't they,
as a favourite coat becomes like you, and becomes you?

Every Story Tells It All

The way I see it, I might be planning a seduction, – arranging the table, choosing the music and the drinks, subduing the lights – but this is more a ritual of summoning, of waiting, of questioning, of simply hoping for the new fleet of words to arrive on the white roadstead of the page. But not a sail is in sight, nor a funnel, nor a flag. Perhaps something is wrong with the air tonight? Yet it seems no more pestilential than usual, and since to wait is to be powerless, I light a cigarette in homage to you, my words. Ah, words! – equally skilled in arias, ensembles and rustic choruses yet sometimes intractable and wayward as friends can be when you have just given them all your best advice: inevitably they go off next day and sleep with *that* person again, – they shower them with undeserved sweetness!

It is still high summer in October. The windows are open and the outside comes in with a fire-truck for a calling card. Stop! I don't believe I wrote this. I had intended to fill each page of this writing with *Profitable Wonders*, and here I am complaining about the noise as if life were a party in the next house to which, by some unpardonable oversight, I have not been invited. This will get us nowhere. What's the use of complaining, borrowing a philosophical hair-shirt, cultivating that toad-like bottom-of-the-well feeling? I won't! But what next? What can stop this small void from widening like the hair-line crack in the foundations that soon threatens to bring down the improbably tall tower of our longing?

Well, we might discuss the failings of poets, the way they punch the air full of holes with their questions and can't come up with a single serviceable answer, the way they'll compare anything to something and something to anything. How must novelists feel looking at the scraps, the lyric wisps these poets run off perhaps in half an hour on a Thursday afternoon, between a phone-call and the T.V. news? A poet gives you a tie-pin, a novelist gives you the complete suit and the shoes. This afternoon I can't accrue the lumber of a novel, but a story might begin to tell itself, unrolling like a landscape scroll. Stories have a way of keeping ideas in their place, and how easily a plot will carry you along over the most difficult obstacles, – it is the perfect canoe, motor powered, built for white water!

There was a man. He looked up at a gold-capped, Byzantine tower in New York City when the sun made it a miracle at early evening. That is too elaborate, of course, – he simply saw this thing gleaming like the sun, and for no reason felt like crying. Then he glanced at the palm of his left hand and saw a scale of gold attached to it. Next day there were two more scales. He didn't think much of it at first. He worked for a law firm in a minor position. He was lucky. He had a good apartment with a bathroom not actually *next* to the dining table. A couple of days later he noticed more scales on the palm of his right hand, and so it went on for several weeks until his hands began to glitter so brilliantly that people in the office couldn't help but notice. He explained that it was a skin complaint for which he was receiving treatment. Any time his palms were upturned light was refracted off the ceiling. He dissembled and kept his hands in his pockets when he could. He tried gloves for a while. The infection spread along his forearms but his shirts covered it. At last it reached his throat and his face. He could no longer deny his transformation. He was still young and as the gold spread over his body he felt he was entering into a state of perfect health and balance. But problems soon set in. Though his appearance was by now astonishingly beautiful those about him were shocked and repulsed by the change. His period of health and near-euphoria was short-lived. He began to lose sensation, as if he were, indeed, a metal. At last he became so rigid it was impossible for him to walk to his place of work. He found that he no longer needed food or drink. He consented to become a statue, – merely the idea or ideal of a man – and in time was placed in a corner of Union Square, guarded by a trench and a barbed-wire fence. As civic order collapsed in the final years of the century he proved impossible to preserve. He was broken into pieces and distributed among many families. In the years that followed gold lost its value. A fragment of his arm or heart wouldn't buy you even half a loaf.

This, I think, is the whole of the story, the one I had been wanting to tell you all the time. Or is it? It is obvious we cannot

116

end here, since a story cannot provide that sense of general, all-conclusive cadence we require. Furthermore it had been my original intention to tell you about today, – the very day on which the story of *The Golden Man* occurred to me as I was walking east along 23rd Street through the rain. And further, I wanted to tell you about this moment, this *now* in all its uniqueness. But as soon as I write it the moment slips backwards under my hand. As they pass these moments accumulate behind me, towering up like a pile of cabbages on a stall. Sometimes I am able to reach back, take one of them and translate it into words. I doubt that my translations are ever faithful to the original. Each moment must be joined into a mesh of other past moments which may never before have encountered each other, to make a new here-and-now on the page which the future shadows as a beech tree shadows a sundial. But a kind of vertigo afflicts us if we think too much about time and the words run out of control. My story may stand for an attempt to halt all movement forward through time, to freeze the blood in its veins, to stop the heart without consenting to death, yet we are also reminded that a statue may fall victim to human needs and compulsions, and vanish utterly. Of the statues of Praxiteles only one remains, I think, his *Hermes Carrying the Infant Dionysus*, and even this is incomplete: the bunch of grapes held up to amuse the infant god is missing, as are the arm and hand that held it.

If all else fails (*has* failed) I can at least describe a place. This seems to offer some stability, for while it is true that certain European monuments have been taken to pieces, shipped and reassembled in America we may be reasonably sure that the ground they once stood on remains. Besides I do not want to describe ancient monuments or great cities, but only the room in which I write. I would like to exclude all elements of narrative from my description. I would also like to exclude all elements of metaphor, but this will be difficult: we only have to look at a thing for it to become metaphorical. A rose is never a rose. This isn't of much importance as we go about our lives, – doing the laundry, laying down lures for roaches and the like, – but it is surely of some importance and, on occasion, may seem crucial, threatening you with a kind of "referential mania" in which the very air coming in through the window carries a specific message intended for you alone. You do not want to receive it. It is too much. And it can get worse. Even the dark spots on the carpet become animate and flash blackly.

At times like this you start desperately counting the bricks in the wall just to have something certain and fixed in your life. Let me assure you this is not something I plan to do now. Nor do I want to present you with a mere catalogue of the room's contents and measurements, although this would be one sure way of avoiding metaphor. A longer focus is preferable as a beginning. Imagine that a camera suspended from some giant boom tracks in toward the southern end of Manhattan. It is evening and the western sky is ablaze, – and look how many lights are coming on to welcome us! It is one of a thousand routine transfigurations. We descend into the street and approach the door of the building ... Or perhaps you have travelled from the north along the valley of the noble Hudson, a passenger on *The Storm King*, *The Maple Leaf*, *The Sleepy Hollow* or *The Niagara Rainbow* and you have just arrived by cab from Grand Central, but in any case you are now approaching the door. It opens easily...

Not so fast! The approach itself must be described. To get to the door you must first climb five broad steps each painted the same dull, turquoise colour. At the topmost step you should pause since this is no ordinary doorway. On either side are pilasters crowned with capitals in the Corinthian style, both somewhat clumsily modelled. At the base of the right-hand pilaster is a man's bearded face. His expression is fierce as if he were designed to discourage unwanted callers. In the lofty parlance of the architectural decorator's trade he is called *The King*, and at the base of the left-hand pilaster we should find the face of his consort, *The Queen*, but where this should be there is only an ugly smudge of plaster. I imagine that the face of *The Queen* was intended to balance the "guardian-monster" aspect of the king and that she must have worn a smile of such graciousness it was like a bouquet pressed into the visitor's hand. Above the lintel of the door are two more faces, one the soft face of a youth or a young woman, the other an older man's face sporting the extravagant moustache of a Parthian horseman. These faces are smaller and framed by what may be wings or stylised palm

118

branches. (They are wings becoming branches or branches becoming wings.) One wonders why it was considered necessary to guard the doorway of a modest, tenement building with such a congery of images. We seem to be looking at the emblems of an allegory whose meaning has been lost to us. Yet there is no real sense of loss: these builders were not classical masters, but however casually or myopically they may have leafed through the dictionary of available forms it is good that they felt that their building required the dignity of ornament, for ornament is richness, not superfluous luxury.

We must now hurry on past the gaping mouth of the king, through the first door and the second door, along the narrow corridor (hardly wide enough for two people to pass) up the stairs and, – quick now! – open the third door and you are, at last, *home*! But the word is at once too resonant. How it echoes! Your room becomes a cavernous, vaulted cathedral and in the distance racks of candles burn before the images of archangels whose faces are those of forgotten aunts, uncles and cousins. You think of the house where you were born, the place where you spent your happy or unhappy childhood, its gardens, parks and fire-escapes. The colour jonquil may come to haunt you because this was the colour your first bedroom was painted, or you may remember the terrible day your sister was taken away to the sanatorium. And you go further, you begin to meditate on the remote origins of your family or race, – in the forests of Germany, in Italy's desolate south, on the west coast of Africa or in the province of Shantung. In rapid succession you also see vivid scenes from all the apartments, houses, towns, or cities in which you lived at various times in your life and for a second the recollection of an ordinary street may bring tears to your eyes. How far away the word "home" has taken you! You are suffering from a species of mnemonic vertigo, even though the medical profession may not acknowledge such a condition. Your mind seems to have become a slide-show operated by a hyperactive child. Calm yourself, it will soon end. It is no use crying out "Oh why did I leave?," you know your reasons were good and this momentary bout of misery is factitious as if you owed it to someone, – your mother perhaps? But she requires that you be happy, so for heaven's sake *shape up*! You are an adult after all (as much as anyone ever is) and you left "home" a long time ago. In this sense homesickness is an incurable illness; however, it is not fatal. You will go on living, and this has to be the best place for you. It is a room.

Of walls and floors and ceilings there is the usual complement, but the windows are many, six in all. You may imagine that it is daily flooded with light like a conservatory or sun room, but you would be mistaken since fully four of these windows open on to a narrow air shaft which offers only an all-too-immediate view of more walls and windows (over thirty windows in all) and in attempting to see the sun in that direction you could break your neck. The windows that matter are the two that face to the street and the south. But there is a problem. On the opposite side of the street a tall building rises like a tombstone blocking the sun which can only enter obliquely, early or late. Yet this is enough since, when sunlight enters it extends itself like a lounging odalisque across a broad, carpeted window-seat. No odalisque myself I don't lounge there much but like to look in that direction as I sit at my desk working. And that invaluable instrument, the telephone, is never far from my hand. I think of the days before the invention of the telephone as a prolonged Dark Age. How did people organize their lives? How was friendship cultivated? The telephone is an instrument to be played like a saxophone. It is a conduit to delight, bringing me the voices I want to hear, not the voices that are pressed in upon me from the street or a neighbouring apartment, – dissonant marginalia clamouring for position.

On certain evenings it is only raising a barrier of music that I can feel alone and situated at the centre of myself. I take a cassette and feed it to the black machine, and the barrier rises, – a reef, a vertical aviary, a contrapuntal thorn-hedge infested with white blossom. Imagine these imaginary flowers drooping over the broken keys of my piano. This is not the mythical beast Mandelstam described with its "*golden veins and eternally inflamed bone.*" It is not the enormous piano of the nineteenth century, visited by tempests, ravens and moonlight, nor yet the aloof and ghostly piano of Busoni, nor the terraced and mirrored pianos of Debussy and Ravel. It is not even the humble piano of the schoolroom abused by hymn tunes and Czerny. Incapable of the simplest,

120

nearly mindless sonatina, it is a black, scuffed silence. No doubt if I threw it out I would have room for a comfortable sofa, but this I will never do. It is a useless, ugly thing you say. Not so. Besides if we did not make room in our lives for things we have no immediate use for how drearily the days would pass, like holes punched in a card. No one would buy flowers, for what could be more useless than flowers in a vase? And poetry is useless like a paper raincoat, someone would say, and music also. If nevertheless I have found a use for music that is not principally why I value it. When I am writing to the accompaniment of music I feel that the music is somehow *there* on the page, tangled in the words like the cord in a curtain. It goes without saying that the words cannot translate the music. Even if I set out to do such a thing, how could I succeed? It would be like trying to convince roses of their intelligence. And how many futile pages would it take to make explicit the exact ambiguities of a single chord?

We value music because of its ability to *say something and not say it*, and so it can sometimes seem that everything has been said, that for a moment we have heard The Whole Truth and will now be able to face the approaching years with a new understanding, crystalline and very nearly mineral in character, it is so close to the essence of things. Alas, the moment is already gone and we cannot say what it was we thought we heard in the sounds. But our melancholy instructs us nonetheless in ways of which we may be unaware, and envy can drive us to achieve things of which we never believed ourselves capable. To make a poem that sounds "musical" is the easiest thing, but if you truly admire music, if you are passionate and enquiring with regard to it this can never satisfy you. You will be filled with the preposterous desire to make a poem that is "like music" on the levels of thought, structure and meaning. You – to whom a score is Chinese characters – cannot succeed. It will be like building a Versailles or a Fontainebleau without knowledge of the first principles of architecture or landscape gardening, but if, amid the resulting confusion, you manage to raise one colonnade before a mob of autumn trees you will have succeeded beyond all hope. And rather a great failure than a small success. A suburban villa may be good to live in but in the realm of the imagination it is better to be the author of ruined cities. Remember the words of the song: *The very difficult I will do right now, the impossible will take a little while.* Should anyone call you crazy it is the highest tribute. So do not scorn my piano. The poor mute isn't deaf after all, and in its silence is a *Concert of Angels*.

On days when music fails me I am invaded by the noise of a hundred true and sorry stories. You could say, "To live in New York is to inhabit the cell of a monstrous hive," but I prefer not to look at it that way. How many inveterate city-dwellers have penned tedious effusions concerning the virtues of nature! May they chew grass. To confuse beauty with virtue must be some kind of crime, since both have their distinct existence. And why close your eyes to what is at hand? Rivers and mountains are fine in their way but they spring few surprises. It is not madness that surprises us in the city but sanity and courtesy, – the way people and their vehicles take pains to avoid collisions, the way pleasantries and apologies are exchanged without a second thought, the way help is given. It is here, under stress, we learn our manners and amid *Babylonian chaos* learn the value of artistic order. Of course you cannot regiment your life according to this *Idea of Order*, but a white porch rises like the porch of a temple next to an acre of trash and is enhanced by this proximity; towers commune with clouds and trees with paving stones.

Granted, an apartment in New York is not a place for anchorites, and if it is yet a refuge, in the sense that the public masks don't have to be worn here, it does not offer escape. The law of mutability governs it. It is a room, and discounting unforeseen disasters will not collapse about my head, yet it is full of evidence of change, and in its very gradual way moves forward in time like a sailing ship the winds have all but deserted, but still it moves though its captain does not know where its destination might lie, – which is to say this is not the room it was at the turn of the century. Then it was several rooms, or so a palimpsest of moldings and irregularities in the ceiling seems to suggest. It may be typical of our time for one large, airy space to be preferred to several smaller, dimmer ones. We do not seem to want the different departments of our lives to be divided too strictly from one another, and yet conversely we all seem to be concerned to retreat to our corners, pulling our special environments close around us like blankets, huddling down with our movies and our music. At the same time we have more opportunities than ever before to circulate widely and freely, and we seize these opportunities and are glad that they seem to be endless, or nearly so like the *Arabian Nights*.

It is probable that at all times the outside world has seemed at once inviting and hostile. Just how inviting or hostile depends on the particular time. For example, at the beginning of the ninth century A.D. the young poet Li Ho, while residing in the splendid city of Ch'ang-an, wrote a famous poem called *Don't Go Out the Door* (such at least is the title of the English translation I have before me). It is a kind of "worst case scenario." He warns us that Heaven is inscrutable and Earth keeps its secrets. If we should take a step beyond the door "nine-headed monsters" will eat our souls, frosts and snows will snap our bones, and dogs will be set on us sniffing and snarling "until the end of all afflictions." In other words, you'd better stay put, fix yourself a drink, because you're liable to get mugged out there. That isn't a city you're looking at, it's an ice cave full of crushing black light, and those aren't people, inhabitants of this borough, they're lost souls, participants in a wind-swept pantomime. *De profundis clamavi.* You come up from this nightmare within a nightmare within a nightmare with the bends and a pain like an arrowhead lodged in your skull. You open the hatch of your bathysphere and breathe in: the air is surprisingly fresh. The dust and fumes have settled, retreated to some other state. And the thought of all that space at the heart of the continent is neither menace nor promise: in theory, it could become anything a sufficiently large number of people wanted it to be, if only a concordance were published.

Countless days of light and shade have come and gone through the windows. No evil is intended. You have shut the door. The world will have to do without you for today. It will manage perfectly well, and so will you. It is good to sit at home in a large city and think of all the things you could be doing that you have decided not to do. For now, *you have more important private concerns.* You need not feel confined. Here are the literatures and musics of the world, and to go from the window-seat to the piano and thence to the desk and the bed, and to walk from there briskly past the disorderly dining table until you arrive at the kitchen and the bath can be quite a journey, involving discoveries of a surprising, almost archaeological nature. It would be easy now to reconstruct the history of last week if you so wished. At last you return to the desk with its invitingly blank page. You adjust the angle of the gooseneck lamp and gaze briefly at the postcards that, for you, take the place of household gods: Kafka in an oval frame, Martha and the Vandellas in beehives, "Baghdad on the Hudson," a sunset over the same river. The pen touches the paper and the world – *your* world at least – is once again in rapid motion. You are intoxicated by the thought of the destinations that await you. If this were a river you would relish the challenge of the rapids and the floating branches. You cease worrying whether this movement is movement forward toward "sure obliteration" and "the end of all afflictions," since you may equally well be speeding backward towards some luminous, nearly forgotten episode you now wish to fix forever in the amber of a sentence. At the same time you are moving out into space, freely circulating, and the configurations of stars assume the shape of stanzas awaiting your transcription. You are alone in your room and so surrounded by companions whose words delight you. (And music glides across the water. Is it Mozart or Poulenc? Surely it is not the boring *Water Music* of Handel.) In other words, you are where you have always wanted to be, and the years hover about you like a cloud of feathers. Soon you will make a pillow of them and sleep for a while. In your dream the tulip tree's single, unseasonal flower becomes a mass of bloom, a candelabrum of petals.

Much can be achieved within the limits of a room, yet nothing will be achieved if you do not, on occasion, open the door and step out with the firm conviction that something agreeable is likely to happen to you. Between staying in and stepping out there must be balance. What is the point of waiting for fear and sorrow to take up residence on your doorstep as they surely will like "gaunt, pariah dogs" if you do not make some effort to get out and discover how they make their passage through life, touching everyone as they go? Better you should find their lairs than they yours. I am not of Pascal's persuasion. I go out often with friends to explore the radiant evenings that occur here-abouts. In the grid of the streets I find enjoyment and instruction. I become filled with the desire to move about and cultivate many encounters, and still to remain loosely anchored here in these words. Words, – my distraught, adored, obstinate musical nota-tion limping out from the raised curtain of the left margin! Oh palaver of tall reeds, oh tolling heart! The time will come to aban-don all you have won and begin again, in doubt.

Notes: Translations, Transcriptions and Mistranslations

1. *From Lorca's Letters*. Virtually all the material for this sequence derives from *The Selected Letters* of Lorca as translated by David Gershator and published by *New Directions*. I had been asked to write a review of the book, but since I do not know Spanish and am no Lorca scholar I was unconvinced that I was the right person for the task. I began by filling a page with all the phrases, sentences and paragraphs that most appealed to me, and very soon forgot about the review. The Lorca fragments seemed determined to form themselves into poems. Some sections of the sequence derive from only one or two letters, while others are composed from widely scattered fragments. Once I had the material I wanted I did not refer back to the original letters but combined and rephrased different fragments very freely. As this process continued I added some lines of my own, but there is very little that is not related closely to Mr Gershator's translations.

2. *The Wonderful Tangerines*. This sequence is based on the bizarrely designed sleeves of classical recordings on obscure labels bought 'for a song' in Manchester. No. 1 is a Haydn symphony, No. 2 Dvorak's Piano Concerto, No. 3 Brahms' Hungarian Rhapsodies and Bartok's String Quartets, while No. 4 is the same composer's *Bluebeard's Castle*. My title derives from a mistranslation of the title of Bartok's second ballet *The Miraculous Mandarin*.

3. *The Sky My Husband*: the name of a boutique in Paris.

4. *Four Poems After Li Ho*. These versions of the Late T'ang poet Li Ho are the result of a collaboration with Tsung Woo Han. Our versions are sometimes very free, sometimes very literal. I am not sure that they should be regarded as translations, but in all cases we have attempted to remain faithful to Li Ho's extravagant and haunted imagination. Each English couplet represents a single line in the Chinese with the exception of the last lines of *Ballad of The Old Men and The Blue-Jade Water* where one line has become two couplets: the possible implications of a single phrase in the Chinese became too alluring to resist.

5. The word *heilignüchterne* occurs in Hölderlin's *Hälfte des Lebens*, – a poem that also inspired the finale of Hans Werner Henze's Seventh Symphony. The translator in question is Christopher Middleton.